Also by Ric Edelman

The Truth About Retirement Plans and IRAs

The Lies About Money

The Truth About Money

Ordinary People, Extraordinary Wealth

Discover the Wealth Within You

The New Rules of Money

What You Need to Do Now

RESCUE YOUR
MONEY

HOW TO INVEST YOUR MONEY
DURING THESE TUMULTUOUS TIMES

Ric Edelman

Simon & Schuster Paperbacks

New York   London   Toronto   Sydney   New Delhi

Simon & Schuster Paperbacks
An Imprint of Simon & Schuster, Inc.
1230 Avenue of the Americas
New York, NY 10020

First Simon & Schuster trade paperback edition July 2016

SIMON & SCHUSTER and colophon are registered trademarks of Simon & Schuster, Inc.

For information about special discounts for bulk purchases, please contact Simon & Schuster Special Sales at 1-866-506-1949 or business@simonandschuster.com

The Simon & Schuster Speakers Bureau can bring authors to your live event. For more information or to book an event contact the Simon & Schuster Speakers Bureau at 1-866-248-3049 or visit our website at www.simonspeakers.com.

Interior design by Ric Edelman and Christine Janaske

Manufactured in the United States of America

10 9 8 7 6 5 4 3 2 1

Library of Congress Cataloging-in-Publication Data is available.

ISBN 978-1-5011-5276-4
ISBN 978-1-4391-5806-7 (ebook)

*According to *Barron's*, "The formula [used] to rank advisors has three major components: assets managed, revenue produced and quality of the advisor's practice. Investment returns are not a component of the rankings because an advisor's returns are dictated largely by each client's risk tolerance. The quality-of-practice component includes an evaluation of each advisor's regulatory record." The rankings are based on the universe of applications submitted to *Barron's*. The selection process begins with a nomination and application provided to *Barron's*. Principals of Edelman Financial Services, LLC self-nominated the firm and submitted quantitative and qualitative information to *Barron's* as requested. *Barron's* reviewed and considered this information, which resulted in the rankings. "The Top 100 Independent Financial Advisors" was published Aug. 27, 2012; Aug. 28, 2010; and Aug. 31, 2009. "The Top 1,000 Advisors Ranked by State" was published Feb. 18, 2013; Feb. 20, 2012; Feb. 21, 2011; and Feb. 22, 2010.

NOTE TO READERS

This book is dedicated to all those who, despite being apprehensive about investing, are convinced that financial security and prosperity can be theirs if someone will simply show them the way.

Acknowledgments

Millions of Americans are impulsively making bad investment decisions. You need solid and effective advice, and you need it delivered in a quick, clear manner.

The advice you're looking for is in your hands.

I am indebted to my firm's financial planners for their assistance in the development of this book, to my supervisor of creative services Christine Janaske, staff editor Mike Lewis, and portfolio manager Mitch York.

Thanks go to Simon & Schuster and my editor, Ben Loehnen, and, as always, my agent, Gail Ross.

Most important is my wife, Jean. Her love and support make everything I do possible.

Contents

Overview: The Secret to Successful Investing

What is the secret to successful investing? If you're like many Americans, you've sought the answer. Indeed, there's no shortage of ideas. Stocks, bonds, mutual funds, exchange-traded funds, real estate, options trading, commodities — you've encountered dozens of ways to invest. You've also tried some of them.

An investment in knowledge always pays the best interest.

— *Benjamin Franklin*

And they've all led you to the same place: this book.

After all, if any of those ideas had made you rich, you wouldn't be reading this page right now.

I've seen a lot of people like you in my three decades as a financial planner. You're careful with your money, and you want it to grow. You've tried a lot of ideas, maybe even worked with a broker or two (or three), but nothing seems to have worked.

That's okay. It's even common. Throughout the 30 years my firm has been managing billions of dollars for people just like you, I've spent a lot of time studying investment strategies and learning how consumers get it wrong and what you need to do to get it right.

And I have exciting news for you! I've found the secret to successful investing, and I'm sharing it with you in this book. The secret is so clear, so obvious, and so easy that you'll kick yourself for missing it all these years. To find out what that secret is, all you have to do is turn the page.

Buy
Low

Sell
High

Uh-oh. I suspect you're feeling a little disappointed. Maybe even a little annoyed. I paid how much for a book that tells me to buy low/sell high? You've got to be joking.

Indeed, you are probably hoping — even assuming — that I am joking. Everyone knows you're supposed to buy low/sell high. And everyone also knows the line is a joke, because everyone knows it can't be done.

But it's really true. The key to investment success really is buying low and selling high. And in this book I really am going to show you how to do it.

To help you understand how to do it correctly, I'm also going to show you:

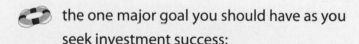 the one major goal you should have as you seek investment success;

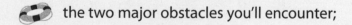 the two major obstacles you'll encounter;

the one big question you'll have to face; and

 the two basic "truths" that confront — and confound — every investor.

In the short time it takes you to finish this book (I bet you can read it cover to cover in one sitting), you'll know how to construct a portfolio that can help you obtain above-average returns, below-average risks, and below-average costs.

So let's get started.

One Major Goal You Should Have

When people seek investments, they tend to have one goal in mind: They want to beat the market.

Don't agree? Then tell me why you compare the performance of your investments with the S&P 500 Stock Index. You're gauging your success by comparing your investment results with the overall market, as measured by the S&P 500, the Dow Jones Industrial Average, or some other stock-market index.

If you're beating the market, you're happy. If you're not, you're unhappy.

Guess what? Trying to beat the market is the wrong goal.

In fact, that's a disastrous goal. Taking that approach sets you up for failure.

Why? It's really very simple. And we need look no further back than 2008 to understand why. In 2008 the S&P 500 lost 38.5%.*[1] If you lost only 30%, congratulations! You beat the market!

Somehow I doubt you (or your spouse) would be thrilled at such news.

Thus we must remember that "beating the market" isn't the point. In fact, only one thing matters when it comes to investing: achieving financial security. *That* is your one major goal.

The sources for all statistics can be found on page 175.

Think about it. The purpose of investing is to help you achieve your goals, whether that means sending your kids to college, retiring comfortably, or caring for aging parents. It's financial security that matters, not some benchmark that has no relevance to your personal life.

People who focus on the stock market are missing the point. You need to emphasize your goals.

CHAPTER

TWO

The Two Major Obstacles That You'll Face

If financial security is the goal, you'll soon encounter a couple of problems. Let's explore them.

Obstacle 1: Taxes

The first obstacle you'll encounter is taxes.

When you earn money from your occupation, you pay income taxes.

When you purchase goods, you pay sales taxes.

If you invest money, you'll pay income taxes on the interest you earn or capital gains taxes on the dividends and profits you receive.

If you buy real estate (and in some jurisdictions, cars, boats, and airplanes), you'll pay property taxes.

If you give money to family members, you (not they) might owe gift taxes.

And if you should die with more money than Congress or your state government feels is appropriate, your estate will pay estate and/or death taxes.

As everyone who has accumulated money knows, money does not solve every problem. But it sure does create new ones.

**FIGURE
2.1**

Top Tax Rates
as of January 1, 2016
(percent)

Federal Income Tax	**39.6**
Federal Capital Gains Tax	**23.8**
State Income Tax	**13.3**
Estate Tax	**40.0**
Gift Tax	**40.0**
Local Property Tax	**2.9**
State Sales Tax	**7.5**

Sources: Internal Revenue Service and the Tax Foundation.

Obstacle 2: Inflation Erodes Your Buying Power

The second obstacle to financial security is harder to notice (because you never actually write a check for it, the way you write a check to the IRS), but it's just as damaging.

It's inflation.

As it rises, it erodes the buying power of a dollar.

As shown in Figure 2.2, inflation has averaged 3.0% since 1926. Since 2003, it has averaged 2.2%. Sometimes it's higher, as when it averaged 8.6% from 1973 to 1974. But at other times it's quite low. From 2010 through 2015, it averaged only 1.5%. But over long periods, it's been remarkably consistent at 3.0%,[2] so that's what you should assume when engaging in long-term financial planning.

FIGURE
2.2

Inflation Is
a Fact of Life

Since 2003 **2.2%**

Since 1983 **2.8%**

Since 1926 **3.0%**

CPI for All Urban Consumers. Source: Bureau of Labor Statistics.
Data through December 31, 2015.

Why Those Who Invest "Safely" Often Go Broke

The sad truth is that taxes and inflation most hurt the people who know the least about investing.

Let's assume you place $100,000 into a five-year bank certificate of deposit that pays 0.8% annually. That was the average CD rate as of December 31, 2015, according to bankrate.com.

If you earn 0.8% on $100,000, you earn only $800 in interest. And you don't keep all that because the interest is taxable.

Let's assume you pay both federal and state income taxes. Let's further assume your combined federal/state tax bracket is 30%. Because the CD paid 0.8%, you lose 0.24% to taxes, leaving you with a profit of 0.56%.

And let's not forget inflation. If inflation is 0.7%, as it was for the year ending December 31, 2015, you'd actually be losing 0.14% on every dollar you invested in that CD. Now, losing 0.14% annually might not seem like much, but if you lose 0.14% every year for 20 years, guess what happens? You end up losing 2.8% of your money. In other words, if you start with $100,000, over 20 years you'll watch your money "grow" to $97,200 in real economic terms.

However, that loss amount is deceivingly low. That's because inflation has rarely been as low as it was during 2015. Between 2010 and 2015, it averaged 1.5%. Since 2005, it has averaged 2.3%. And since 1926, it has averaged 3%. So let's use 2.3% inflation for purposes of this illustration. On that basis, as Figure 2.3 shows, you'd have lost 1.74% of your money for each of the 20 years, for a total loss of 34.8%, leaving you with a balance of just $65,200 after 20 years.

To understand the crisis this presents, consider the couple who both retire at age 65. They've spent years — two full, lifelong careers — accumulating their savings, and they know the money they have is all the money they will ever have. If they lose it, it's gone. They know they don't have another 35 years to regenerate their savings if they lose it. So they invest carefully, choosing investments that can't lose money. They reject the stock market as too risky and instead place their life savings into bank CDs or the like.

FIGURE
2.3

How Taxes and Inflation Affect You

Five-year CD	**0.80%**
30% Tax Rate	**− 0.24%**
	0.56%
Average Inflation	**− 2.30%**
Annual Result	**− 1.74%**
	x 20 yrs
20-year Result	**− 34.8%**

$100,000 invested today would be worth only $65,200 in 20 years.

Earnings reflect hypothetical return, not meant to reflect any specific investment. Taxes based on 30% combined federal/state income tax rate. Inflation rate is based on the average for the Consumer Price Index from 2005 through 2014 according to the Bureau of Labor Statistics. Past performance does not guarantee future results.

And for a while, things seem okay. Thanks to their pensions, Social Security, and the interest they earn from the CDs, they have an annual income that meets their needs. Everything seems fine.

But let's fast-forward. In 20 years (or more likely sooner), they will discover that their strategy has failed them. You see, at 3.1% annual inflation, the cost of living doubles every 23 years. As a result, it takes twice as much income at age 88 to buy the same goods and services they bought at age 65. They need more money.

But most pension checks (for those lucky enough to get them) don't increase. Annuity payments never do. Social Security checks notoriously rise less than the average inflation rate (and in 2010, 2011, and 2016, there was no increase at all).

Do you know any retirees in their seventies, eighties, or nineties who say they don't have as much money as they need? Chances are, they were financially "fine" 20 or so years ago.

If you limit yourself to investments that don't keep up with inflation, you could find yourself in a serious financial predicament in the future. You'll discover that the cost of everything has doubled, but your income hasn't.

That's what happens when you plop the bulk of your money into low-yielding investments. You'll go broke, safely.

And that's the irony. The people who are putting their life's savings into bank CDs and the like do so because they want safety above all else. They don't want to put their money in the stock market because they fear losing money. They're afraid to invest in real estate. They don't understand foreign securities. So they choose things like bank accounts, which (they think) offer safe, predictable, and stable rates of return.

Predictable and stable, yes. Safe, no.

As a result, millions of Americans are going broke safely. And they don't even know it.

The Minimum Return You Must Earn

This is why you must overcome the long-term impact of taxes and inflation.

To see exactly how much you must earn merely to break even, relative to taxes and inflation, look at Figure 2.4 on the next page. It shows how much you must earn, based on your combined federal and state income tax bracket and the current rate of inflation.

For example, if inflation is 3% and you are in the 30% combined federal/state tax bracket, you must earn 4.3% just to break even. If your investments are earning less than that, you're losing money in real economic terms.

This leads to just one question: Where can you earn more than the minimum return indicated in Figure 2.4?

FIGURE
2.4

Just to Break Even

Here's the minimum return you must earn based on taxes and inflation.
(percent)

If you pay this in federal and state taxes...	...and the inflation rate is...				
	3%	4%	5%	6%	7%
	...you must earn at least:				
10.0	3.3	4.4	5.6	6.7	7.8
12.5	3.4	4.6	5.7	6.9	8.0
15.0	3.5	4.7	5.9	7.1	8.2
17.5	3.6	4.9	6.1	7.3	8.5
20.0	3.8	5.0	6.3	7.5	8.8
22.5	3.9	5.2	6.5	7.7	9.0
25.0	4.0	5.3	6.7	8.0	9.3
27.5	4.1	5.5	7.0	8.3	9.7
30.0	4.3	5.7	7.1	8.6	10.0
32.5	4.4	5.9	7.4	8.9	10.4
35.0	4.6	6.2	7.7	9.2	10.8
37.5	4.8	6.4	8.0	9.6	11.2
40.0	5.0	6.7	8.3	10.0	11.7
42.5	5.2	7.0	8.7	10.4	12.2
45.0	5.5	7.3	9.1	10.9	12.7
47.5	5.7	7.6	9.5	11.4	13.3
50.0	6.0	8.0	10.0	12.0	14.0

You won't do it by investing in bank checking or savings accounts, money market funds, bank CDs, T-bills, government savings bonds, life insurance, or fixed annuities.

Despite this fact, millions of Americans have placed trillions of dollars into those investments. They then wonder why they aren't able to keep pace with the cost of living, and they demand that Congress do something about it.

Too bad they don't realize that the solution is in their grasp. Fortunately, by reading this book, it's in yours.

Literally.

Investments That Can Generate the Returns You Need

If putting all your money into bank accounts won't provide you with investment success, where can you generate the returns you need?

Consider where your money is. Ask yourself if those bank accounts, insurance products, or investments can produce the returns you need over the next 30 years. And when you do, focus on the fact that you're investing for a lifetime, not just for a year or two. So focus on the average returns earned over a lifetime of investing.

THREE

One Big Question

Okay, so now you know you need to earn higher returns than those offered by bank accounts and the like.

You have only one question: How do you earn those returns?

It's simple. And I've already told you the answer.

Buy low/sell high.

Market Timing — aka Buy Low/Sell High

Lots of people try to buy low/sell high by engaging in "market timing." That's when you buy investments you think are about to rise in price, and you sell investments you think are about to fall.

There's only one problem: Market timing doesn't work; I know of no case or study showing that anyone has ever achieved long-term success doing it.

But there *is* a massive, long-term study showing that investors lose huge amounts of money by trying.

The study is Dalbar's 21st Annual Quantitative Analysis of Investor Behavior. It clearly shows that mutual-fund investors earn only a portion of the returns earned by the funds they invest in.

Wait a minute.

How can there be a difference between what a mutual fund earns and what its investors earn?

After all, if you own a mutual fund that rises 10%, your account rises 10%, too. Right?

Not necessarily.

That's because mutual-fund performance is reported on a calendar basis. But you don't actually invest on January 1 and sell on December 31.

Instead, you buy and sell on random dates during the year. The result: Fund investors don't own their funds for the exact period that investment results are reported by mutual-fund companies.

And, for many investors, those buy/sell dates aren't random at all: The average investor puts money into mutual funds (they buy) when they think prices are going to rise, and they take money out (they sell) when they think prices will fall.

Dalbar shows that investors consistently get it wrong — they have lousy timing. The analysis is clear:

Investors consistently buy *after* prices have risen, and they consistently sell *after* prices have fallen.

As a result, millions of investors wind up with returns that are far lower than what they'd have gotten if they had simply held their shares for the entire year.

This is demonstrated by Figure 3.1. It shows that the average diversified stock fund gained 8.3% in 2014, according to Morningstar. But Dalbar's research shows that the average investor return was only 5.5% — proof that investors bought while prices were higher and sold while prices were lower. Consequently, on average, stock fund investors earned only two-thirds of the returns that their funds actually produced.

And it's not just stock fund investors who blow it. In 2014 (excluding municipal and TIPS funds, which were excluded from Dalbar's study because they are taxed differently), the average bond fund investor earned only 1.2% while Morningstar says bond funds earned an average of 3.1%. Bond fund investors got only 39% of the profits their funds produced!

FIGURE
3.1

Investor Returns vs. Investment Returns
2014 Results

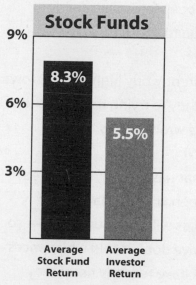

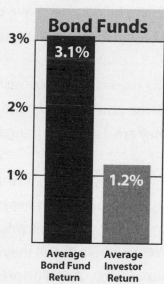

Sources: Dalbar's Quantitative Analysis of Investor Behavior, 2015 and Morningstar.

Even worse, Dalbar and Morningstar show that 2014 was not an aberration. Indeed, Figure 3.2 reveals that over the past 30 years, the average diversified stock fund gained 10.7% per year, but the average investor in those funds earned only 3.8% per year, or 36% of the return.

Clearly, investors have been engaging in market timing for decades, have been failing miserably at it — and foolishly continue to try.

The reason people consistently buy high and sell low — the opposite of what they're trying to do — is that they are doing two things wrong:

1. They think that what has recently happened will continue to happen. If prices have recently fallen, they think prices will continue to fall — so they sell. But all they've done is sold while prices are low. And if prices have recently risen, they think prices will continue to rise — so they buy.

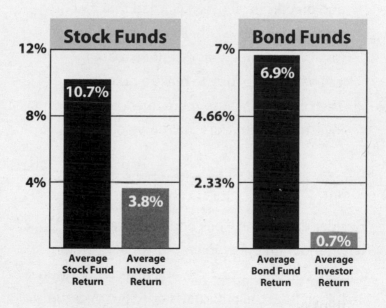

Investor Returns vs. Investment Returns

30-Year Results

1985-2014

Stock Funds

12%

10.7%

8%

4%

3.8%

Average Stock Fund Return

Average Investor Return

Bond Funds

7%

6.9%

4.66%

2.33%

0.7%

Average Bond Fund Return

Average Investor Return

Sources: Dalbar's Quantitative Analysis of Investor Behavior, 2015 and Morningstar.

But all they've done is bought while prices are high.

Sold low, bought high.

Bad combination.

2. They sell low and buy high because of fear and greed, respectively. Worried that recent declines will persist, they sell to avoid further losses. Or, excited that recent increases will persist, they buy to make a quick buck. Their emotions cause them to engage in investment behaviors that prove costly.

There are many examples of this behavior.

Consider the trading week ending December 5, 2008. That Monday, the Dow Jones Industrial Average dropped 680 points, or 7.7%, and investors withdrew $16 billion from their mutual funds.[3] But over the next four days, as the Dow rose 6%, investors added

$4 billion to their funds, according to the Investment Company Institute (ICI).

They sold low and bought high.

They did the exact opposite of what they should have done.

Want a more recent example? Consider the month of August 2015, when the Dow declined 6.4%, its worst-performing month in more than five years, its worst August performance since 1998, and its sixth worst-performing month overall. The S&P 500 fell 6.3%, its biggest monthly drop in three years and worst August performance since 2001.

During the week starting Monday, August 24, the Dow experienced several wide swings, but the biggest occurred that Monday, when it plunged more than 1,000 points within two minutes after opening. Many investors panicked and began liquidating their stock positions, creating the second most active trading day of all time, pulling $11 billion out of stock funds, according to ICI. But the only thing those panicked investors managed to do was sell at a low, because that 1,000-point drop on Monday marked the low point of the entire week. By liquidating, they merely locked in their losses.

That August week (in fact, the entire month) gave me an opportunity to say something I hadn't said since 2008: The market's decline created one of the best buying opportunities in years.

If you contribute regularly to your 401(k) or other retirement plan at work, you should be glad when such buying opportunities come along. It essentially means everything's on sale, so you're buying more shares for less — and this can pay off for you down the road.

For proof, consider what ICI and the Employee Benefit Research Institute found when they looked at the results of 26 million Americans who had a 401(k) plan at year-end 2007 and still had one at year-end 2013. Of the 26 million, only four million kept contributing to their plans on a consistent basis during the entire period — even during the Credit Crisis of 2008 when the market lost as much as 65% of its value before recovery began in March 2009. The other 22 million stopped contributing during the market's decline.

The survey (released in September 2015) found that, as of December 31, 2013, the group that contributed regularly throughout the six-year period saw their accounts increase by an average of 16% per year — four times greater than those who had stopped contributing.

Want still more proof? On October 15, 2014, the S&P 500 (which had just hit an all-time high the month before), dropped by 9.5% — just short of the 10% needed for Wall Street to call it a "market correction." An analysis by SigFig found that one out of five investors were spooked and sold some or all of their stocks. The study then found that, as of August 21, 2015, those who had sold 90% or more of their stocks the previous October posted the worst returns of all investors during the ensuing months. That group's returns were down 19% for the period, while those who sat tight and held on to their positions were down only 3.7%.

This demonstrates the foolishness of trying to buy low/sell high the way most people try to do it. And believe it or not, I'm actually going to show you how to do it right and how to do it easily.

But to fully understand what I'm about to show you, we need to examine other ways investors (you?) have tried to achieve success. By studying how others fail, as we've been doing, we can better appreciate the correct approach.

Following the Fads

Instead of trying to figure out when to get in or out, some investors try to invest in the latest fad. There's always one or more. In the 1990s it was tech stocks. During the beginning of the 21st century, it was real estate. When the economy began to falter in 2008, it seemed like everyone was talking about oil and gold. Then "green" (environmental) stocks were in vogue.

What you need to understand is that fads and investing go hand in hand. As long as there have been investments, there have been fads. The first documented fad, in fact, was the Tulip Craze of 1636. At its height, a single tulip bulb sold at auction in the Netherlands for today's equivalent of $75,000.[4]

If you think it's impossible for people to pay high prices for worthless items, then you've never heard of Beanie Babies.

The Tulip Craze wasn't the only time people paid crazy prices for investments. In 1720, Sir Isaac Newton — generally regarded as a pretty smart guy — was among the many who lost a fortune speculating in the stock of the South Sea Company. Now known as the South Sea Bubble, the speculation ended when the stock's price fell 84%.[5]

During the Roaring Twenties, the Dow was up 497% at its peak on September 3, 1929. The market then fell 48% by November 13, hitting bottom on July 8, 1932, with an 89% loss.[6]

Nelson Bunker Hunt and William Herbert Hunt tried to corner the silver market in the 1970s and managed to get the metal to rise 566% from 1979 to 1980. The price of silver then fell 77% by 1982.[7]

Then there was the Japanese stock market, which rose 3,100% between 1965 and 1989. But in 2015, 26 years later, the Nikkei Index was still trading at less than half that number.

Then came Internet mania. From 1994 to 2000, the NASDAQ Stock Market Index jumped 627%. After prices peaked on March 10, 2000, the index went on a three-year decline, falling 77% by October 9, 2002.[8]

The next fad to emerge, then crash was real estate. From 2000 to 2012, the S&P/Case-Shiller Home Price Index grew sharply, but as with every fad before it, the trend ended swiftly and dramatically, resulting in a deep and prolonged recession.

The real estate debacle didn't satiate investors' hunger for the next fad. For a time, foreign stocks (led by the so-called BRIC nations of Brazil, Russia, India, and China) were all the rage, as were gold and oil, both of which reached all-time highs in 2008 before falling sharply.

The fascinating aspect of fads is comparing the rises in their prices with the dates investors bought and sold. For example, tech stocks started rising in 1994 — but most of the money that was placed into dot-coms was invested in late 1998 and 1999, well after the bulk of the profits had already been made.[9]

Ditto for the real estate boom. Prices peaked in 2003, but *home sales* peaked in 2005.[10] All those who bought houses in 2004 and 2005 missed the profits but caught the subsequent losses.

Why is it that people tend to invest in fads *after* the prices have already risen?

The reason is simple: You didn't invest in Internet stocks in 1994 because you hadn't heard about them. It was only in 1998 — after prices had tripled — that tech stocks were featured on the evening news and magazine covers. Likewise, real estate wasn't news in 2000 — but it was in 2004, after people started telling stories about the profits they had earned.

Thus, we buy into fads after prices have already risen simply because that's when we hear about them. It's another example of buying high/selling low.

FIGURE
3.3

Fads Might Boom,
But They Always End in Busts

Event	Boom to Bust	At the Peak	At the Bottom
Tulip Craze[1]	1634–1636	+2,000%	−99.9%
South Sea Bubble[2]	1719–1720	+695%	−84%
The Roaring Twenties[3]	1921–1932	+497%	−89%
Silver Market[4]	1979–1982	+566%	−77%
Japanese Market[5]	1965–1992	+3,100%	−57%
Internet Mania[6]	1994–2002	+627%	−77%
Real Estate Boom[7]	2000–2012	+107%	−35%
Oil Boom[8]	2001–20??	+733%	−75%??*

*At the writing of this book. [1]Source: UCLA, 2006; [2]Source: L. D. Neal, "How the South Sea Bubble Was Blown Up and Burst: A New Look at Old Data," in E. N. White, ed., *Stock Market Crashes and Speculative Manias*, 1996; [3]Source: stockcharts.com; [4]Source: Bloomberg; [5]Nikkei Stock Index. Source: Ibbotson Associates; [6]NASDAQ. Source: Ibbotson Associates; [7]S&P/Case-Shiller Composite — 20 Metro Home Price Index; [8]Bloomberg WTI Crude Oil Spot Price.

So if you want to successfully invest in a fad, all you have to do is to buy it before you've ever heard of it.

Ummm, let's try that again.

In other words, people fail to make money in fads because by the time they hear about it, it's too late: The profits have already been obtained.

Investing in fads is simply not a successful investment strategy.

Do You Trust the Media?

The media certainly offer us plenty of investment advice, often with scary headlines about the investment climate.

On November 14, 2012, a headline in *Forbes* magazine warned: "Market Selloff after Obama's Re-election No Accident; Recession Coming." The article stated, "Now that the election is over, stocks are dropping with no bottom in sight. This is no accident, given investors' fears of higher taxes and continued big spending . . . we are headed for a recession."

Well, actually there *was* a bottom in sight — the very next day, after that article appeared! On November 15, 2012, a post-election stock rally began. As you may recall, stocks rose throughout 2013, with the S&P 500 posting a gain of nearly 30% for the year — its best in 18 years. The Dow Jones Industrial Average ended 2013 up 26.5%, and the tech-focused NASDAQ gained a whopping 38%. The increases continued, though to a lesser extent, through 2014.

Do you remember the *sequester*? That term refers to $1.1 trillion in automatic federal budget cuts from March 1, 2013 through 2021, affecting many federal spending programs.[11] Before the law took effect, there was intense speculation over whether Congress would agree on a deal to stop the automatic cuts.

The media, of course, helped to rattle investors' nerves. For example, on February 28, 2013, a

Wall Street Cheat Sheet headline said, "Stock Investors Spooked by Sequestration Fears." The article said, in part, "After having been ignored for most of the week by U.S. investors, sequestration spending cuts moved to the front burner with a steep sell-off into the market close."

As it turned out, that "front-burner" status lasted all of one day. The March 1 sequestration deadline came and went without a deal to stop it, but investors didn't care: Stocks rose 2% the first week of March. Prices were up 10% by mid-May and continued to steadily climb for the rest of the year, posting the double-digit gains mentioned earlier.[12]

And who can forget the *fiscal cliff*? The media used that term so often during 2012 that it eventually topped the Lake Superior State University 2013 List of Banished Words.

The phrase referred to laws scheduled to come into effect in January 2013 — simultaneously increasing taxes while cutting spending. On November 7, 2012, a *USA Today* headline said, "Fiscal Cliff Now Market's Big Worry." The story said "investors are nervous about the market and don't want to feed it capital because they don't know what the rules of the road are going to be."

But in reality investors weren't nervous at all. From November 7 through December 31 — the day Congress reached a compromise to avoid the fiscal cliff — stocks actually rose 2.3%, according to Wyatt Investment Research.

This wasn't the first time the media got it wrong in their efforts to scare us.

Worried about "The Aging Bull Market," the March 11, 1996, cover of *U.S. News & World Report* shouted, "INVESTOR BEWARE!"

I'm not sure what we were supposed to beware, because the Dow gained 17.5% from then to the end of the year. The Dow gained another 27% in 1997, 25% in 1998, and 18% in 1999.[13]

In August 1997, *Money* magazine screamed, "Don't Just Sit There . . . SELL STOCK NOW!"

Hope you didn't listen, because the Dow, then at 7694, rose for the rest of that year and the next two.

Fortune magazine's cover on September 28, 1998, predicted "The Crash of '98," citing "the bouncing Dow" and "a troubled world" as support for its prediction.

Of course, *Fortune* was wrong. There was no crash in 1998. Nor, for that matter, in 1999. Instead, stock prices kept rising.

But prices finally did begin to decline in March 2000 and kept declining for two and a half years. That brings us to October 2, 2002.

On that day, apparently, *USA Today*'s editors couldn't take it anymore. After all, the Dow had fallen 45% since March 2000. So page 1 of the paper's Money section asked, "Where's the Bottom?" with a subhead stating, "No end in sight as day by day Dow sinks away."

With the benefit of hindsight, we now know when the bottom occurred. It was October 2, 2002 — the very day *USA Today* asked the question.

What about CNBC's Jim Cramer, who offers a barrage of advice on TV? Consider these examples:

On November 20, 2012, Cramer urged investors to sell two stocks immediately: Hewlett-Packard and Best Buy. But just over six months later, Hewlett-Packard was up 115.6% and Best Buy had gained 124.6%.

At the end of that six-month period, BBY was the third-best performer among the 749 stocks in the Wilshire US Large-Cap Index, and HPQ came in fourth. The probability of being so wrong on two of the four best performers was 1 in 35,062, according to *CBS MoneyWatch*.

It's also interesting to note that, in his book *Getting Back to Even*, published in October 2009, Cramer included Hewlett-Packard among 12 stocks in a chapter on how to invest for the recession recovery. Between then and his November 2012 recommendation to sell that stock, HPQ lost 73.8%. Thus, investors who followed Cramer's advice both times would have lost almost three-quarters of their investment and later missed out on more than doubling it.

On the Wilshire index for the same six-month period (November 2012–May 2013), the two top-performing stocks ahead of BBY and HPQ were Netflix, with a 174.5% gain; and Green Mountain Coffee, with a 161.7% gain. But Cramer advised selling Netflix on November 2, 2012, and selling Green Mountain on September 30, 2012. But by April 23, 2013, after Netflix's big gain, Cramer recommended buying it.

What are the odds of making four sell recommendations on what ended up being the four best performers out of 749 stocks? An amazing 1 in 13.1 billion, according to *CBS MoneyWatch*.

Earlier, when the Wall Street investment firm Bear Stearns was on the verge of collapse in 2008, Cramer predicted, "No, no, no, Bear Stearns is fine!" But just a week later Bear Stearns was out of business.

Cramer's mania can sometimes be astonishing to witness. On Friday, June 27, 2008, a day after the Dow fell 358 points, he wrote in his daily online column, "Sell everything. Nothing's working. Revisit when the prices are adjusted for a big recession, soaring inflation, and a crushed consumer. Sell at 12,000 and come back at 10,000. Even better: Short it."

Then, just two business days later (Tuesday, July 1), in a column titled, "10 Reasons the Rally Could Last," Cramer wrote: "This is a real turnaround from hopelessness, while it will be hard for the bears to believe that they might actually be on the receiving end of the pain. I have to believe that it can last for more than one day."

What had happened between Cramer's Friday panic (sell everything!) and Tuesday's euphoria (this is a real turnaround!)?

Apparently, nothing: On Monday the Dow had gained three points.

What about other financial pundits?

Consider Charles Nenner, a market analyst who previously worked for Goldman Sachs and other firms. He created what he calls the "Nenner Cycle" system that is supposed to predict major market movements. Nenner claims his system warned him of the 2008 crisis.

A fundreference.com article references a July 15, 2010, interview with Nenner that was reported on with headlines such as "Charles Nenner: Dow Headed to 5,000, Get Out While You Can!" In the interview, Nenner was quoted as saying, "It is going to be a very difficult few years to make some money . . .

I don't expect the economy to pick up until 2020." At the time of his prediction, the Dow stood at 10,359. Within five years, the Dow was up 70%.

On September 12, 2011, CNBC reported that Harry Dent was predicting that the Dow (then at 11,061) would fall below 10,000 in the near term before crashing to around 3,000 in 2013. Instead, the Dow enjoyed a gain of 26.5% by year-end 2013 and reached 18,000 by 2015 — six times higher and in the opposite direction than Dent had predicted.

Ahead of the 2012 presidential election, *MarketWatch* columnist Paul Farrell predicted the markets were headed for a crash regardless of the election result. Just over a year later, in his column dated December 21, 2013, despite the market's stellar year, he wrote that "after the exuberance of the 'Christmas rally' passes, reality will set in." That column was headlined "Doomsday Poll: Still a 98% Risk of 2014 Stock Crash." Instead, the Dow gained 7.5% in 2014, and the S&P 500 and NASDAQ were each up more than 11%.

But my favorite example of all comes from *Money* magazine. In March 1994, the publication's cover touted "Eight Top Investments That Never Lose Money."

By the end of the year, seven of them did.

The examples are endless; an academic study showed that investors who follow media recommendations lose, on average, 3.8% of their money in the following six months.[14]

Clearly, trusting the media's investment advice is not a successful strategy. Yet judging from the millions of people who read, listen, surf, and watch all the commentaries, it's also clear that most people don't know this.

Not-So-Expert Advice

If we can't trust the media to help us make good investments, we should at least be able to consult the experts, right?

The problem is that the experts rarely agree.

At any given moment, on any given issue, you can find many experts predicting one result and just as many predicting another. In fact, with so many thousands of economists, market analysts, portfolio managers, and traders, each year is certain to find *someone* who correctly predicted the topic du jour.

Problem is, it's almost never the same person twice.

There aren't many people who would invest their life savings on the prognostications of a sportswriter — we all know their predictions are highly unreliable — yet millions invest their money based on the musings of a single money manager.

For example, Marc Faber, a Swiss investment advisor and author of the *Gloom, Boom & Doom Report*, has made numerous bearish forecasts over the years. In an interview with CNBC in April 2014, he predicted a 2014 market crash, saying "I think it's very likely that we're seeing, in the next 12 months, an '87 type of crash." But the market actually ended 2014 in fine shape.

Earlier, Jason Trennert, *USA Today*'s "top strategist for 2008," predicted that stock prices would rise 14% in 2008. Instead the S&P 500 fell 38.5%.

(As bumbling TV spy Maxwell Smart would say, "Missed it by *that* much.")

With all the golf swings made every year, *someone* is going to hit the ball into that little hole for a hole in one. With all the baseball games played every year, *someone* is going to pitch a no-hitter. Sports fans know that the hole in one won't necessarily be hit by the best player, nor will the perfect game be pitched by the best pitcher. But *someone* will do it.

Sometimes people get it right. Sometimes they get it wrong.

We know sportswriters get it wrong. Why, then, don't investors know that an investment analyst or portfolio manager might be wrong?

And why are so many people willing to invest their life savings on the prognostications of such a person?

Predictions are not reliable in sports or on Wall Street.

Don't rely on experts.

Don't Count On Quality

Many investors, daunted by the challenge of picking the right investments, simply default to the oldest, biggest, best-known, and most popular companies in America, such as those listed in Figure 3.4. How could you go wrong with that?

Take a company like Marathon Oil. Founded in 1887, it is one of the best-known oil companies in the United States. Based in Houston, it carries out production and exploration activities in the United States, Europe, and Africa.

Marathon Oil is in the S&P 500 Stock Index. Its stock, like that of the other major oil companies, has performed well over the years, but if you owned Marathon Oil stock from 2014 through October 2015, your shares would have lost 63% of their value, as Figure 3.4 shows. The shares lost 53% in 2015 alone.

Or you could have invested in Hewlett-Packard. As Figure 3.4 shows, its stock fell 63% in the two years from 2011 through 2012.

IBM stock lost 22% from 2014 through October 2015.

Alcoa stock lost 42% from 2011 through 2012 and 74% in the five years from 2008 through 2012.

Best Buy stock lost 46% in 2012 alone and 63% from 2011 through 2012.

H&R Block stock lost 45% in 2010.

Goodyear stock lost 45% during the 10 years from 2001 through 2010.

Are the Best-Known Companies Really the Best Investments?

FIGURE
3.4

Company	Stock Performance	Period
Marathon Oil	53% loss in 1 year	2015
	63% loss in 2 years	2014–2015
Macy's	45% loss in 1 year	2015
Bed Bath & Beyond	37% loss in 1 year	2015
Walmart	26% loss in 1 year	2015
American Express	24% loss in 1 year	2015
	21% loss in 2 years	2014–2015
Caterpillar	23% loss in 1 year	2015
Mattel	32% loss in 1 year	2014
	37% loss in 2 years	2014–2015
Best Buy	46% loss in 1 year	2012
	63% loss in 2 years	2011–2012
Netflix	61% loss in 1 year	2011
Bank of America	58% loss in 1 year	2011
Goldman Sachs	45% loss in 1 year	2011
Citigroup	44% loss in 1 year	2011
	86% loss in 10 years	2006–2015
H&R Block	45% loss in 1 year	2010
Staples	36% loss in 2 years	2014–2015
IBM	22% loss in 2 years	2014–2015
Chevron	22% loss in 2 years	2014–2015
Hewlett-Packard	63% loss in 2 years	2011–2012
Alcoa	42% loss in 2 years	2011–2012
	74% loss in 5 years	2008–2012
Staples	51% loss in 5 years	2011–2015
Southwest Airlines	53% loss in 10 years	2002–2011
Goodyear	45% loss in 10 years	2001–2010

Source: S&P 500 and Dow Jones Industrial Average as of January 1, 2016.
Past performance does not guarantee future results.

Clearly, investing in a large, well-established company does not mean you are immune from suffering massive losses over extended periods of time. Yet millions of Americans entrust these companies with their future financial security.

As a financial planner who has counseled thousands during my career, I have seen lots of people make this error. They invest their life savings into a single stock: that of their employer. Others invest most of their money into a single company because they like its products. This mistake is so common that I've given it a name: *Enron-itis*.

In 2001, Enron was ranked seventh on the Fortune 500 list of America's largest companies.

That was the year it went broke.

It was also the year of my first television appearance on *The Oprah Winfrey Show*. Oprah asked me to counsel a woman caught up in Enron's collapse.

A former mid-level employee of the company, she had more than $2 million in Enron stock in her 401(k) account. When the company went broke, she lost both the $2 million and her job.

Those Enron employees were not unique. People continue to suffer by investing in the stock of their employers. Debacles such as WorldCom, Conseco, Global Crossing, United Airlines, US Airways, General Motors, Lehman Brothers, and more haven't dissuaded millions of employees from placing too much money in the stock of their employers. Fidelity said in 2013 that more than 15 million people owned a combined $400 billion worth of company stock via their employer retirement plans.

And people are still doing it today. *Morningstar* reports that more than 70% of the money in the 401(k) plan operated by supermarket chain Publix is invested in company stock. The same for Sherwin-Williams. And the figure is over 50% for 19 other companies, including Colgate-Palmolive, ExxonMobil, Dillard's, Chevron, McDonald's, and Lowe's.

Whether it's your own employer or a company you feel you can trust because of its age, size, and reputation, do you really want to risk your financial security on the fortunes of a company over which you have limited knowledge (even if you work there) and no control? Clearly, that's a foolish bet.

You cannot count on quality for your financial security.

Hot Sectors That Aren't

Some investors recognize the foolishness of investing in specific stocks.

After all, even though the airline industry will survive, that doesn't mean every airline will.

Therefore, some investors conclude, it's better to select a broad-based sector of the stock market instead of a single company or even a single industry. They figure it's better to split stocks into two categories, such as growth stocks and value stocks.

Or large companies and small companies.

Or U.S. stocks and foreign stocks.

Then, they figure, you just invest in the one group that will do better than the other.

But how do you do that?

It's a question many investors try to answer.

It's impossible.

The performance of all these groups from 2000 through 2015 is shown in Figures 3.5 through 3.7.

As you can see, in any given year, one beats the other.

But it's impossible to predict which one will do better the following year.

And yet, many investors insist on trying.

FIGURE
3.5

Growth Stocks vs. Value Stocks
2000–2015

2000	Value
2001	Value
2002	Value
2003	Value
2004	Value
2005	Value
2006	Value
2007	Growth
2008	Value
2009	Growth
2010	Growth
2011	Growth
2012	Value
2013	Growth
2014	Value
2015	Growth

Source: Morningstar. Past performance does not guarantee future results.

FIGURE
3.6

Large Stocks vs. Small Stocks
2000–2015

2000	Small
2001	Small
2002	Small
2003	Small
2004	Small
2005	Large
2006	Small
2007	Large
2008	Small
2009	Large
2010	Small
2011	Large
2012	Large
2013	Small
2014	Large
2015	Large

Source: Morningstar. Past performance does not guarantee future results.

FIGURE
3.7

U.S. Stocks vs. Foreign Stocks
2000–2015

2000	U.S.
2001	U.S.
2002	Foreign
2003	Foreign
2004	Foreign
2005	Foreign
2006	Foreign
2007	Foreign
2008	U.S.
2009	Foreign
2010	U.S.
2011	U.S.
2012	Foreign
2013	U.S.
2014	U.S.
2015	U.S.

Source: Morningstar. Past performance does not guarantee future results.

FOUR

The Two "Truths" That Prevent You from Investing Successfully

So far we've learned that market timing doesn't work. Nor should you follow fads, trust the media, rely on so-called experts, or make big bets on blue-chip stocks or hot sectors.

None of these ideas works, yet many investors persist in relying on these strategies. When one fails, they move to the next, believing (or merely hoping) it will pay off.

Why do investors do this? Because they believe in two basic truths:

1. Stock prices rise and fall.

2. The stock market is risky, volatile, and unpredictable.

Do you agree with these statements?

Let's explore them.

Basic Truth 1: Stock Prices Rise and Fall

Of course, literally speaking, this statement is true. But it's misleading. That's because the statement is incomplete; it's not really accurate to say that stock prices "rise and fall."

Oh, sure, on any given day, prices might rise or fall. But over long periods, it's more accurate to say that prices in the overall stock market rise *a lot* but fall *a little*, as shown by Figure 4.1. (By the way, this is the most important chart in the book.)

FIGURE
4.1

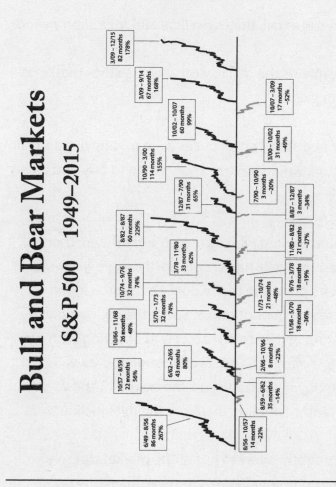

Bull and Bear Markets
S&P 500   1949–2015

3/09 – 12/15	82 months	178%
3/09 – 9/14	67 months	168%
10/02 – 10/07	60 months	99%
10/90 – 3/00	114 months	155%
12/87 – 7/90	31 months	65%
8/82 – 8/87	60 months	229%
3/78 – 11/80	33 months	62%
10/74 – 9/76	32 months	74%
5/70 – 1/73	32 months	74%
10/66 – 11/68	26 months	48%
6/62 – 2/65	43 months	80%
10/57 – 8/59	22 months	56%
6/49 – 8/56	86 months	267%

10/07 – 3/09	17 months	–52%
3/00 – 10/02	31 months	–49%
7/90 – 10/90	3 months	–20%
8/87 – 12/87	3 months	–34%
11/80 – 8/82	21 months	–27%
9/76 – 3/78	18 months	–19%
1/73 – 10/74	21 months	–48%
11/58 – 5/70	18 months	–36%
2/66 – 10/66	8 months	–22%
8/59 – 6/62	35 months	–14%
8/56 – 10/57	14 months	–22%

Source: Ibbotson Associates. Past performance does not guarantee future results.

This chart clearly shows that when stock prices are rising, they rise *a lot* and for a *long time*.

When prices fall, they fall *a little* and for a *short period*.

This explains the real reason why the stock market is able to exist.

Think about it. If stock prices were to only rise and fall, investors would have to know when to buy and when to sell.

Imagine playing with a yo-yo. It goes down, then it comes up. Down, up. Down, up. If that yo-yo were a stock's price, the trick would be to catch it and release it at the right time. But as the chart shows, investing in the stock market is like playing with a yo-yo *while climbing a hill*. Even though the yo-yo is still going down, up, down, up, the height of the yo-yo is constantly climbing, thanks to the hill's incline.

Here's another way to put it: The market doesn't simply go up one point and then down one point.

Rather, it goes up two points, then down one point. Then it goes up four, down one; up three and down one. Sure, sometimes the down is larger than the previous up, but over long periods — 15 years or more, according to Ibbotson Associates — the stock market has always produced net profits. That's why it's wrong to be upset when stock prices fall. Instead of lamenting the current decline, focus on what is about to happen next. This point was particularly important for investors to remember after 2008's terrible performance, and more recently in late 2015 and early 2016.

So if you had the opportunity to invest at the moment of your choosing, where on Figure 4.1 would you choose? Educated investors realize that the best time to invest is at the end of period of decline. In other words, while ordinary investors are upset about market declines, educated investors get excited about them!

So when you notice stock prices are declining, don't be upset. Instead become excited about what lies ahead.

Basic Truth 2: The Stock Market Is Risky, Volatile, and Unpredictable

If you believe this truth, that's because you're familiar with the chart in Figure 4.2. It shows the monthly performance of the S&P 500 since 1926.

Clearly the stock market is volatile. It's also unpredictable. No one can say what will happen next by looking at that chart. And that makes the stock market risky. It's like driving a car blindfolded.

But does this chart really matter?

Think about the last time you invested money; whether you bought a stock, a bond, a mutual fund, some real estate, or added to your retirement account at work — whatever. Now let me ask you a question: When you invested that money, was it your intention to withdraw the money in just 30 days?

FIGURE
4.2

Monthly Performance
of the S&P 500
1926–2015

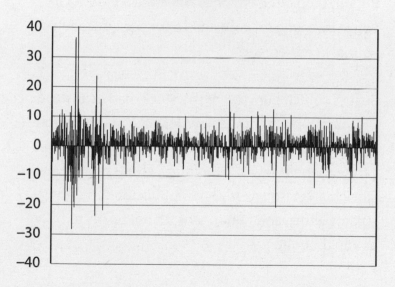

Source: Dimensional Fund Advisors. Past performance does not guarantee future results.

Of course not. Your plan, more likely, was to leave the money alone for years, maybe even decades. So why, then, does the chart in Figure 4.2 matter?

Yet that's how investors — spurred by the media — view the market. They watch it day by day and (in the case of CNBC) moment by moment.

But how could today's price movements matter if you're investing for your child's college education or your own retirement?

So let's stretch our view of the stock market. Instead of a month-by-month review, let's see how it performs over 15-year periods, as shown in Figure 4.3. As you can see, when viewed over long periods of time, the stock market isn't nearly so unpredictable. It's not so volatile either, and that means it's not nearly as risky as you thought.

This is why the best way to view the stock market is over decades — not days, weeks, or months. Invest accordingly.

Fifteen-Year Performance of the S&P 500
1926–2015

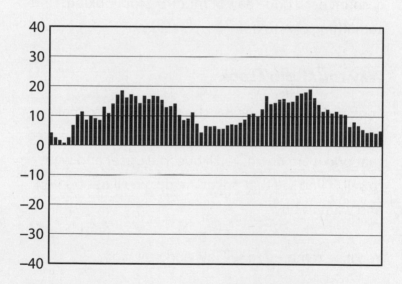

Fifteen-year rolling intervals. Source: Dimensional Fund Advisors.
Past performance does not guarantee future results.

But investors don't understand this. That's why they rip open the envelope as soon as their monthly account statement arrives. In fact, they don't even wait for it; many check prices on the Internet throughout the day.

But if you're seeking to achieve a long-term goal such as college or retirement, why bother looking at your account each hour, day, or month? Stop looking. Find something else to do.

Why You Mustn't Look

Looking often at your investments is likely to make you do the opposite of what you should do. If you see that prices are down, you'll become upset and want to sell. If you see that prices are up, you'll get excited and want to buy.

You'll be tempted to sell low and buy high.

Sound familiar?

A study from Columbia University supports this point: It found that checking your retirement portfolio too often can indeed reduce your returns.

"History shows that the stock market is a relatively safe bet over the long term because it has typically grown," says Michaela Pagel, assistant professor of finance and economics at Columbia. "Investors would be wise to keep this in mind, because those who check their portfolios too often and are driven by daily or hourly fluctuations in the market may make decisions that have a negative impact on their long-term financial prospects."[15]

This is why you must stop paying attention to news about the stock market's activity. The media report only what's happening today, making you think today matters. I've never heard a news anchor say, "As of today, the stock market's average annual return since 1926 years is 10%." Yet that information would be more useful to investors than reporting today's results.

The Truth About the Two Basic Truths

Now you know the truth: The two basic truths are really nothing more than common myths. And by mistaking these myths as truths, Americans set themselves up for investment failure.

Relying on these myths causes people to engage in strategies that don't work, such as trying to buy low/sell high. Following fads. Listening to the media. Relying on experts. Counting on quality. Picking hot sectors.

Dismiss these concoctions and instead believe that the stock market produces profits over long periods. You believe this, after all. Let me prove it to you.

Answer this question:

Twenty years from now, do you believe the Dow will be higher than it is today?

We often ask this question in our seminars. Never has anyone said the stock market will be lower in 20 years than it is at the moment. So I'll assume you also agree the market will be higher in the future.

One more question, if you please.

Take a guess at what the stock market's average annual rate of return will be over the next 20 years. This question is a bit harder to answer, so look at Figure 4.4 for some statistics that might help.

So I'll ask again:

What do you guess will be the market's average annual rate of return over the next 20 years?

FIGURE
4.4

1926-2015	{ *The average return was 10.0% per year.*
1989-2015	{ *The average return was 10.0% per year.*
1990-1999	{ *The average return was 18.2% per year.*
2000-2008	{ *The average return was –3.6% per year.*
2009-2015	{ *The average return was 14.8% per year.*

Data reflect the performance of the S&P 500.
Sources: Dimensional Fund Advisors and Morningstar.
Past performance does not guarentee future results.

As of January 1, 2015, the Dow Jones Industrial Average was 17,823.

If the Dow grows 12% annually over the next 20 years, it will be 171,926 in 2035.

If the Dow grows 10% annually over the next 20 years, it will be 119,904 in 2035.

If the Dow grows 7% annually over the next 20 years, it will be 68,969 in 2035.

If the Dow grows 3.5% annually over the next 20 years, it will be 35,464 in 2035.

The worst 20-year performance for the stock market since 1926 is 3.1%, which would put the Dow at 32,821 in 2035.

The average 20-year performance since 1926 is 11.4%, which would put the Dow at 154,413.

So instead of being afraid of investments, maybe you ought to get excited.

The Secret

Stocks might crash.

Bonds can fail.

Real estate may collapse.

Gold and oil prices can plummet.

Banks can fail.

Money market funds can "break the buck" (lose money and prohibit withdrawals).

Interest rates can reach zero, meaning it can cost more to buy U.S. Treasuries than you earn in interest.

So what's an investor to do?

The answer is simple: Do everything.

As investors painfully learned during the Credit Crisis of 2008, there are times, however unusual, when there is no safe place to hide. Even in normal times, there's always at least one investment doing poorly while others are doing well.

It's easy to talk about what has done well, but no one is able to predict with any consistency what is about to do well.

Therefore, you should buy everything. Do it all.

In other words, diversify.*

When I began my career as a financial planner in the mid-1980s, diversification was an unknown concept for most consumers. By now, you've probably heard about it. But I suspect you don't fully understand it and thus don't know how to effectively execute it.

So let me explain it to you.

Figure 5.1, which is spread across the next two pages, shows how each of 16 asset classes and market sectors performed each year from 2005 through 2015.

Examine each column, and you'll see there is no pattern. It is impossible to predict, based on each asset class or market sector's past performance, whether one will perform better or worse than the others in the following year.

*Diversification does not assure or guarantee better performance and cannot eliminate the risk of investment losses. There are no guarantees that a diversified portfolio will outperform a nondiversified portfolio.

FIGURE
5.1

Asset Class Performance 2006–2015
Ranked 1 (best) – 16 (worst)

	Commodities	Emerging Markets	Oil	Gold	Foreign Stocks	Small Cap Growth	Mid Cap Growth	Large Cap Growth
2006	14	2	16	4	3	8	11	9
2007	4	2	1	3	7	12	5	6
2008	8	15	16	5	14	13	10	12
2009	12	1	2	9	7	5	3	4
2010	8	7	11	4	15	2	1	9
2011	15	16	4	3	14	12	10	7
2012	15	3	16	11	6	9	7	8
2013	14	12	8	16	7	1	5	4
2014	15	13	16	12	14	8	6	4
2015	15	14	16	13	8	9	3	2

Data reflect the Bloomberg Commodity Index, MSCI Emerging Market Index, West Texas Crude, Gold London AM Fixing, MSCI EAFE Index, Russell 2000 Growth Index, S&P MidCap 400 Growth Index, Russell 1000 Growth Index.
Source: Morningstar Direct. Past performance does not guarantee future results.

FIGURE
5.1

Asset Class Performance 2006–2015
Ranked 1 (best) – 16 (worst)

	Long–Term Bonds	Intermediate –Term Bonds	Short–Term Bonds	Small Cap Value	Mid Cap Value	Large Cap Value	Junk Bonds	Real Estate
2006	15	13	12	5	7	6	10	1
2007	8	9	11	15	13	14	10	16
2008	1	2	4	6	7	9	3	11
2009	16	15	14	10	6	11	13	8
2010	12	13	16	5	6	10	14	3
2011	1	2	8	13	11	9	5	6
2012	12	13	14	4	2	5	10	1
2013	15	13	11	2	3	6	9	10
2014	2	7	11	10	5	3	9	1
2015	7	4	6	12	11	10	1	5

Data reflect the Barclays 1-3 Yr US Treasury Index, Barclays US Corporate High Yield Index, Barclays US Govt 5-10 Year Index, Morningstar Long-Term US Treasury Index, Morningstar US REIT Index, Russell 1000 Value Index, Russell 2000 Value Index, S&P MidCap 400 Value Index. Source: Morningstar Direct.
Past performance does not guarantee future results.

There's something amazing about the data on those last two pages, and it's revealed in Figure 5.2: If you had invested equally into all 16 of those major asset classes and market sectors during that 10-year period, you would have earned an average return of 7% per year. But — and here's the amazing part — if you had failed to invest in the three best-performing asset classes of each year, your average return would have been only 2.2%, instead of 7%.[16]

Even though I am regarded as an expert in personal finance, even though my firm manages billions of dollars for people like you nationwide, and even though we've been managing money for more than three decades, I readily admit that my colleagues and I can't predict with any certainty which asset class or market sector will do best next year.

I am willing to admit we don't know. Are you willing to admit you don't know either?

After all, there are only two kinds of investors: those who don't know, and those who don't know they don't know.

FIGURE
5.2

Investing in Thirteen vs. Sixteen of the Markets
2006–2015

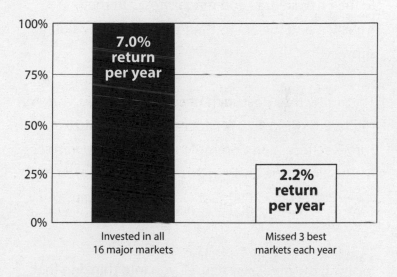

Data reflect the Bloomberg Commodity Index, MSCI Emerging Market Index, West Texas Crude, Gold London AM Fixing, MSCI EAFE Index, Russell 2000 Growth Index, S&P MidCap 400 Growth Index, Russell 1000 Growth Index, Barclays 1-3 Yr US Treasury Index, Barclays US Corporate High Yield Index, Barclays US Govt 5-10 Year Index, Morningstar Long-Term US Treasury Index, Morningstar US REIT Index, Russell 1000 Value Index, Russell 2000 Value Index, S&P MidCap 400 Value Index. Source: Morningstar Direct.
Past performance does not guarantee future results.

It's a Game of Horseshoes, Not a Horse Race

And that's how the personal finance media trick you. You don't know how to pick the right investments, and you know you don't know. The media don't know either. But they know you don't know they don't know. So they pretend they do know (are you getting all this?) so they can trick you, to get you to subscribe to their newsletters and magazines, surf their websites, and tune in to their radio and television shows.

That's why they post such headlines as *MarketWatch*'s "Still a 98% Risk of 2014 Stock Crash" in April 2014, *Forbes*'s "Recession Coming" in 2012, *The Economist*'s "Is This Really the End?" in 2011 and *Veterans Today*'s "Dow Headed to 5,000; Get Out While You Can" in 2010.

In short, the media try to trick you into thinking that investing is like a horse race — that you'd better pick the right horse or you'll be broke.

Because you know you don't know how to pick the right investments, and because the media act as if they do, you follow their advice.

I have good news for you! Investing is not a horse race; it's a game of horseshoes: Being close is good enough to win. Warren Buffett said it best: "It is better to be approximately right than precisely wrong."

Something Else the Media Never Tell You

You probably never noticed: When the media offer hot tips, they never tell you how much risk you're taking by acting on them.

Yet, risk matters — as much as return.

Not sure you agree? Consider this illustration: Driving from Washington, D.C., to New York City typically takes about four hours. If I drove you there in just 90 minutes, would you reward me for my performance or chastise me for the risk I forced you to take? Methinks you'd chastise me.

All investors must balance risk versus return.

You desire high returns. You want to avoid big losses.

To show you how diversification can help you strike the right balance, let's examine the performance of two portfolios during the 15-year period 2001 through 2015. I chose this period because it covers the Credit Crisis of 2008 as well as the bull markets that preceded and followed it.

The stock market is as risky as it gets. Figure 5.3 shows the volatility of a portfolio that's invested entirely in stocks. (Volatility is based on *standard deviation*, which is explained in my books *The Truth About Money* and *Discover the Wealth Within You*.)

Compared to that portfolio is one that invests equally in stocks, bonds, cash, foreign stocks, and real estate. As Figure 5.3 shows, the diversified portfolio enjoyed far less volatility than the one invested fully in stocks.

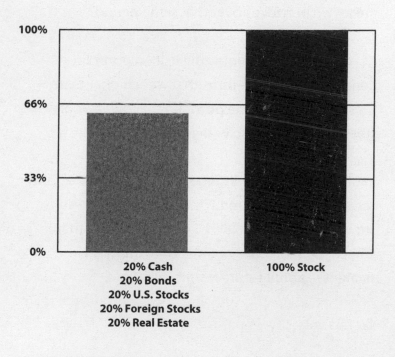

Volatility
2001–2015

100%

66%

33%

0%

20% Cash
20% Bonds
20% U.S. Stocks
20% Foreign Stocks
20% Real Estate

100% Stock

Measure of Standard Deviation. Source: Morningstar Direct.
Past performance does not guarantee future results.

That's no surprise. After all, it's the main reason people diversify: to lower their risk. But some people hesitate to lower their risk, because they fear that doing so will also lower their return.

But that's not necessarily the case! Take a look at Figure 5.4, which reveals the returns generated by those two portfolios over that same period.

As you can see, the highly diversified portfolio generated average returns that were higher than those produced by the portfolio that owned only stocks — and it did so with much less risk.

In other words, lowering the risk does not necessarily mean you get lower returns. (Of course, the results showed in Figures 5.3 and 5.4 are specific to that 15-year period; this is not meant to imply any guarantee about future results.)

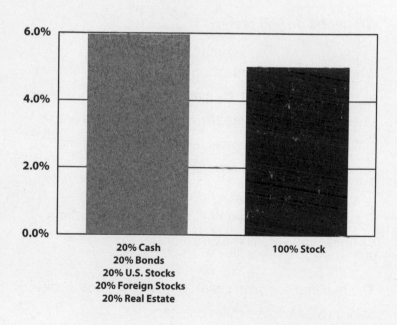

Average Annual Returns
2001–2015

6.0%	
4.0%	
2.0%	
0.0%	

20% Cash
20% Bonds
20% U.S. Stocks
20% Foreign Stocks
20% Real Estate

100% Stock

Source: Morningstar Direct. Past performance does not guarantee future results.

Optimizing Versus Maximizing

To understand this concept, let me offer you two investment choices.

One investment earns 10%.

The other earns 8% but has only half the risk.

Which one do you prefer?

When we pose this question at our seminars, almost everyone prefers the 8% investment. A few, however, say they would rather earn 10% than 8% and are willing to expose themselves to the volatility that seeking such returns requires.

This evaluation is what Wall Street calls portfolio optimization versus maximization.

The maximizer doesn't care (or professes not to care) about risk. He loves roller coasters.

The optimizer cares very much about risk. He doesn't want to throw up during a wild ride.

We've learned through decades of working with individuals just like you that people tend to claim to be maximizers only before they experience the very risks they claim not to mind.

This became particularly apparent in 2008. Many people had no idea they could lose 60% or 70% of their life savings in a matter of months.

And they learned, too late, that they didn't have the stomach for it.

A merry-go-round is a much smoother ride, and it ends up at the same place as the roller coaster — without making you nauseous.

*If you don't know
who you are, the
stock market is a very
expensive place to
find out.*

— *George Goodman, aka Adam Smith*

The Secret to the Secret

Diversification is a proven approach to investment success. Of course, no strategy can guarantee profits or eliminate the risk of investment losses.

So to succeed with this approach, you must apply two crucial elements. Let's explore them.

Crucial Step 1: Maintain a Long-term Focus

You must maintain a long-term focus for one simple reason: It's the only way you can be certain you'll capture the profits that investments offer — and avoid taking the full brunt of occasional downturns.

To illustrate, think about your 401(k) or other workplace retirement plan. Do you contribute to it on a steady, consistent basis — regardless of market volatility or scary headlines?

Well, if you were among those who did during a five-year period that included the 2008 Credit Crisis, you were rewarded for your confidence and fortitude.

The average account balance of workers who participated in their plans consistently from 2008 through December 31, 2012, increased at a compound average annual growth rate of 6.8% — despite a 34.7% drop in their average 401(k) account balance during 2008.

That's according to a study released in July 2014 by the Employee Benefit Research Institute and the Investment Company Institute — similar to but earlier than the one I referenced back in Chapter 3. This report examined the behavior of 24 million 401(k) plan participants and found that a third of them — 8 million people — were consistent participants, meaning that they did not reduce their contributions or shift out of stock funds during that five-year period.

By year-end 2012, according to the study, the average account balance of those people was 67% higher than the average of all participants, and the consistent group's median balance grew 11.9% per year over the period — nearly three times the average for all participants.

These findings match the results of a separate study by Fidelity, released in 2013. It focused on workers who stayed with the same company over the previous 10 years and stayed with the same investments from 2008 through 2012. What happened to their account values? They quadrupled.

The average account balance for those workers jumped 324% over the decade, from $47,100 to $199,800. During the same decade, the S&P 500 rose only 62%.

The secret to their success was Dollar Cost Averaging. By buying in 2008 and 2009, when many others were selling in a panic, they bought more shares with each dollar — and when those shares rose in value, their account values rose dramatically.

Another reason to stay invested over long periods is the fact that the stock market's entire gain for a given year often occurs during a brief window of time. During years when the market is down or flat for the year, it will often recover all or most of its losses during a brief period. Therefore, if you're not invested for the entire year, you could lose all of that year's gains or sustain bigger losses than you otherwise would have.

Figures 6.1 through 6.10 illustrate this.

In our first example, the S&P 500 ended 2015 falling almost 1% — its first negative year since 2008, when it lost 38.5%. But 2015 wasn't a smooth ride. After nearly nine months, the index was down 9%. Had you bailed at that point, you would have realized that loss in your account. However, as Figure 6.1 shows, in just 18 trading days the index was back in the positive before ending the year close to breaking even.

In Figure 6.2, notice that during 2014 (when the S&P 500 index gained 10.6% for the year), 93% of those gains occurred during the final 11 weeks of the year.

Figure 6.3 shows that 2011 was similar to 2015. In 2011, the S&P 500 logged its first 0% performance in six decades, ending the year almost exactly where it started after falling as much as 19% between April and its low on October 3. But it began climbing back, as Figure 6.3 shows, during the final 24 days of trading. Ultimately, the market regained the last 8% of what it had earlier lost.

Now, let's drop back to 2007. As Figure 6.4 shows, the market gained 5.5% that year. But it's worse than you think. That's because from January 1 to November 21, 2007, the market gained nothing. Indeed, the S&P 500 stood at 1,418 on January 1, and it was virtually the same — 1,417 — on November 21.

But then, from November 21 to November 28, the stock market jumped 5.5%. After that, it remained flat for the rest of the year.

We didn't have a good year in 2007 — we had a good week!

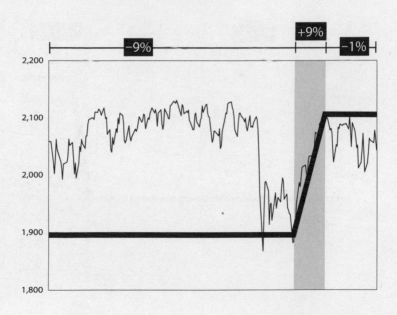

FIGURE
6.1

S&P 500
2015
9% Loss Recovered in 18 Days

Source: Bloomberg. Past performance does not guarantee future results.

S&P 500
2014

93% of Gains Occurred in Final 11 Weeks of Trading

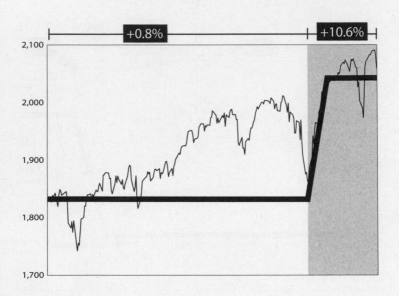

Source: Bloomberg. Past performance does not guarantee future results.

FIGURE
6.3

S&P 500
2011

8% Loss Recovered in
Final 24 Days of Trading

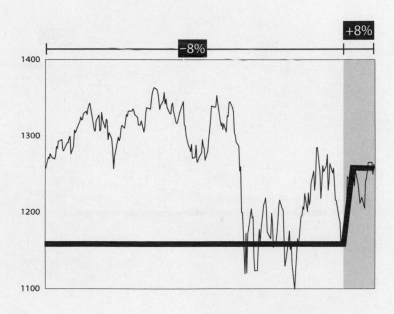

Source: Bloomberg. Past performance does not guarantee future results.

FIGURE

6.4

S&P 500
2007

The Entire Gain Occurred in Just 1 Week

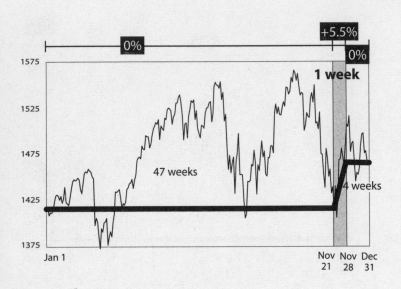

Performance of the S&P 500 Stock Index from January 1, 2007,
through December 31, 2007. Source: Ibbotson Associates.
Past performance does not guarantee future results.

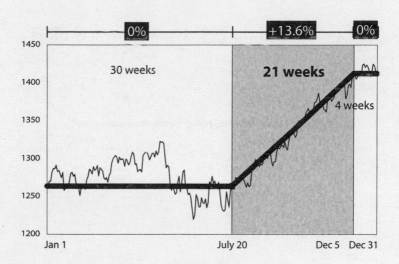

FIGURE
6.5

S&P 500
2006

The Entire Gain Occurred in Just 21 Weeks

| 0% | +13.6% | 0% |

1450

30 weeks

21 weeks

1400

4 weeks

1350

1300

1250

1200

Jan 1   July 20   Dec 5   Dec 31

Performance of the S&P 500 Index from January 1, 2006,
through December 31, 2006. Source: Ibbotson Associates.
Past performance does not guarantee future results.

FIGURE
6.6

S&P 500
2005

The Entire Gain Occurred in Just 8 Weeks

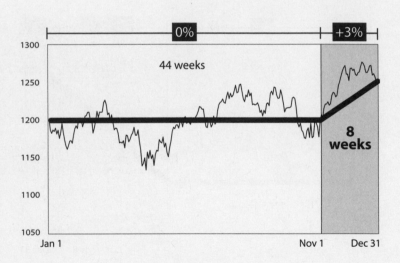

Performance of the S&P 500 Index from January 1, 2005,
through December 31, 2005. Source: Ibbotson Associates.
Past performance does not guarantee future results.

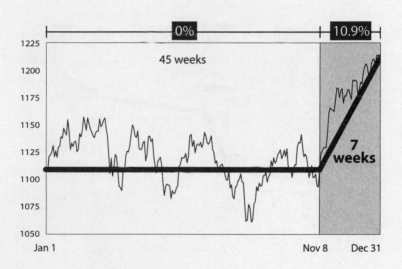

S&P 500
2004
The Entire Gain Occurred in Just 7 Weeks

Performance of the S&P 500 Index from January 1, 2004,
through December 31, 2004. Source: Ibbotson Associates.
Past performance does not guarantee future results.

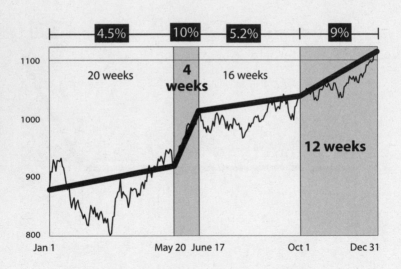

S&P 500
2003
The Entire Gain Occurred in Just 16 Weeks

Performance of the S&P 500 Index from January 1, 2003,
through December 31, 2003. Source: Ibbotson Associates.
Past performance does not guarantee future results.

FIGURE
6.9

S&P 500
1999
The Entire Gain Occurred in Just 22 Weeks

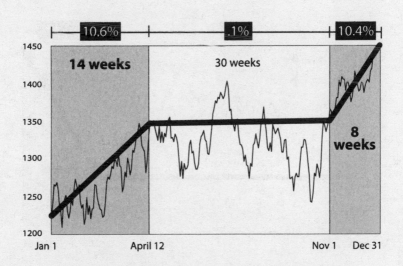

Performance of the S&P 500 Index from January 1, 1999,
through December 31, 1999. Source: Ibbotson Associates.
Past performance does not guarantee future results.

FIGURE
6.10

S&P 500
1998

The Entire Gain Occurred in Just 11 Weeks

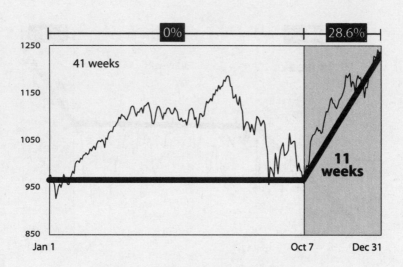

Performance of the S&P 500 Index from January 1, 1998,
through December 31, 1998. Source: Ibbotson Associates.
Past performance does not guarantee future results.

Yet it can be said that 2007 really wasn't that unusual, because we had a similar experience in 2006. As Figure 6.4 shows, the stock market's entire profit of 13.6% that year occurred in a 21-week run.

Similar scenarios occurred in 2005, 2004, 2003, 1999 and 1998 — all shown by Figures 6.5 through 6.10.

You get the point.

In case you don't, I will explain it.

It is common for the stock market to jump in short spurts, followed by long periods of stagnation.

Can you predict when those short spurts are going to occur?

Neither can I. That's why we remain invested the entire time — so we can catch the profits when they come.

Here's another example:

If you were invested in the stock market from 2011 through 2015, you would have earned 10% per year over the market's 1,258 trading days,[17] as shown in Figure 6.11.

But if you missed the best 15 days of that five-year period, your average annual return would have been zero. Yep, the entire profit of five years came in just 15 days.

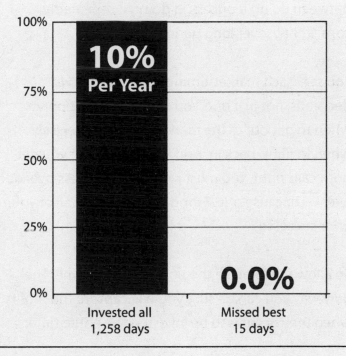

FIGURE 6.11

Why You Need to Be Invested All the Time

S&P 500 2011–2015

Invested all 1,258 days: **10% Per Year**

Missed best 15 days: **0.0%**

Source: Morningstar Direct. Past performance does not guarantee future results.

Could you have picked the best 15 days out of 1,258?

Do you think some magazine columnist or television pundit could have?

Oh, sure, some people manage to make the right call from time to time, getting out at a market top or getting in at a bottom. But there's a big difference between doing it once and doing it repeatedly, consistently, over long periods.

You see, each market-timing call requires two decisions, not just one. You must know not only when to get out of the market, but also precisely when to jump back in. And even assuming you get both calls right, you must repeat the process over and over — because one wrong call wipes out all of your prior successes.

So allow me to make the point one final time: The only way you can be sure you will capture the profits when they occur is to be invested the entire time.

Thus, the first crucial step to achieving investment success through diversification is to maintain a long-term focus.

But how do you do that in the face of a difficult, downright scary economic environment?

You begin by remembering what history teaches us. We've experienced 13 recessions since 1945. The average stock market decline was 40% and lasted 21 months, as shown in Figure 6.12. The longest began in September 1937 and lasted more than five years.

More important, every recession has been followed by a tremendous bull market.

FIGURE
6.12

S&P 500 During Bear Markets

Start	% Return	# Months
September '29	−86	33
March '37	−60	63
May '46	−30	37
August '56	−21	15
December '61	−28	7
February '66	−22	8
November '68	−36	18
January '73	−48	21
November '80	−27	21
August '87	−34	3
July '90	−20	3
March '00	−49	31
October '07	−57	17
Average	**−40**	**21**

Source: Standard & Poor's. Past performance does not guarantee future results.

On average, the S&P 500 has risen 38.1% in the first 12 months of the market's recovery.[18] Furthermore, in the last four recessions, stock prices began rising an average of four months before the recessions ended.[19]

Thus, investors who sell during a decline, thinking they'll wait for the economy to recover before investing again, are almost certain to miss much of the stock market's recovery.

Anyone who says it will take decades for the stock market to reach new highs simply doesn't know what he or she is talking about.

But what if this time is different?

People have been saying that for years. When the stock market crashed in 1987, many people said, "This time it's different."

People said it during the 1991 recession and the bear market between 2000 and 2002.

People also said it when prices were high. In 1999, when I warned on the radio that tech stocks were too high, investors said, "This time it's different." And in 2005, when I said housing prices would not continue to rise, people said, "This time it's different."

No, it wasn't. And no, it isn't this time, either. These times are not different — and the times to come won't be different either.

Yet people insist that every period of extreme volatility is different.

This never proves true.

What is true about recessions, however, is that stock prices rise before the economy recovers. That's because investors can envision profits before they are actually earned. Still, you might ask, if economic weakness is in our short-term future, why not sell and move to cash and wait for the storm to end instead of risking your life savings further?

History provides the reason why you shouldn't do that: Past recessions, panics and depressions have taught us that stock markets recover with astonishing suddenness and velocity. By the time you realize the bottom has been reached, prices have *already* risen sharply — meaning you are forced to buy back in at prices that are higher than when you sold.

The key to succeeding with my advice, then, is *patience*. Another way to state this: You should build your diversified portfolio — and then *do nothing*.

A fascinating study along these lines was published in November 2007 in the *Journal of Economic Psychology*. Scientists examined the behavior of elite soccer goalkeepers during penalty kicks. Although that might seem off-point, the study actually has important implications regarding your investment decisions.

Because the ball in a penalty kick takes only a few hundredths of a second to reach the goal line, the goalkeeper must decide *before* the ball is kicked whether to jump left, jump right, or stay in the middle. Since the study found that the ball is kicked to each of the three areas in equal proportions, you'd assume that goalies do each of the three in equal amounts.

But the researchers discovered that goalies stay in the center only 6.3% of the time.

That seems to make no sense. Why aren't goalies standing in the center more often?

The reason is simple. The goalie knows he's likely to fail; indeed, 80% of the time, a goal is scored. So the fear is not that he'll fail — the fear is he'll look stupid while failing.

Imagine you're the goalie. You're standing on the goal line. The ball is kicked left or right 66% of the time — and you're just standing there. You know what everyone is thinking: *Why didn't you* do *something?*

Thus goalies figure jumping to one side makes it look like they've tried. They feel that action is better than inaction — even though such action actually hurts their results.

The study's authors state, "The action/omission bias . . . has very important implications for economics and management. For example, the action/omission bias might affect the decision of investors whether to change their portfolio (action) or not (inaction)."

In other words, don't just do something, stand there!

Remember my earlier description of what happened on Monday, August 24, 2015? It was the second-most active trading day in market history. The Dow dropped more than 1,000 points during the first two minutes of trading that day. In fact, market volatility that week was huge.

Investors who were glued to CNBC and tracked the market's valuation in real time on their smartphones were probably having panic attacks. Stress levels must have skyrocketed.

I'm sure you'll agree it's not a good way to spend your day. Far better to pay little or no attention. That ensures you won't get upset, which means you won't panic, which means you won't sell while prices are momentarily low. Not paying close attention means you'll *do nothing*. And doing nothing — taking no action and allowing this to pass — keeps you consistent with your long-term strategy.

Unfortunately, thousands of investors didn't do that on that dramatic Monday. Instead they liquidated more than $600 million in stocks and stock funds, moving money into bonds and cash positions. But all they succeeded in doing was selling at a low and locking in their losses.

They should have done what a listener to my weekly radio show did. He emailed me to say, "I recall listening to your program during 2008, when depressed people would call you after seeing losses in their 401(k)s. You'd often tell them, 'Ignore the noise.' At the time I thought that was a rather flippant response, but I gave your suggestion a try and found that it really works! I'm sure my account lost money; I don't know how much, but it doesn't bother me because I know it will be okay in the long run."

This is the advice my firm has given our clients for years:

1. Ignore wild market gyrations.

2. Stay above the occasional fray.

3. Do *nothing* when market volatility occurs.

The alternative is to buy and sell in a frenzy, without really knowing what you're doing or why you're doing it. Perhaps the time Jim Cramer sold on Friday and bought on Tuesday is an example.

That's why, as I said, the first crucial step in achieving investment success through diversification is to maintain a long-term focus.

Crucial Step 2: Buy Low/Sell High

The second crucial step to diversification is to engage in strategic rebalancing.

This step is vital if you're to achieve long-term success. Unfortunately, it's ignored by the overwhelming majority of investors.

The good news: It's easy to understand and even easier to do.

To explain, let's begin with a sample portfolio. In this hypothetical example, we're going to invest equally in stocks, bonds, government securities, and cash, as shown in Figure 6.13.

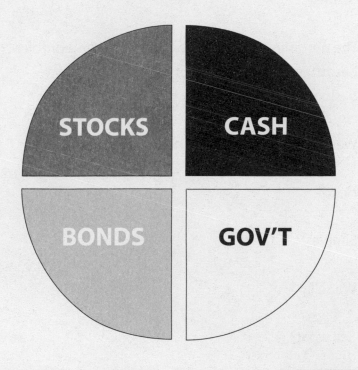

If This Is the Portfolio
We Want . . .

This is a hypothetical illustration to demonstrate the principle of diversification.
It is not representative of the past or future results of any specific investment.

Over time, one asset class will inevitably outperform the others.

Let's assume stocks will be the outperforming investment. You see the results in Figure 6.14: stocks now represent a larger portion of our portfolio than before.

The portfolio is no longer balanced. This is a problem because our portfolio is not allocated the way we designed it. So we must fix it.

We must rebalance the portfolio.

How?

Simple.

We sell.

Sell what?

We sell some stock.

FIGURE
6.14

. . . Then We Need to Rebalance If the Portfolio Later Looks Like This

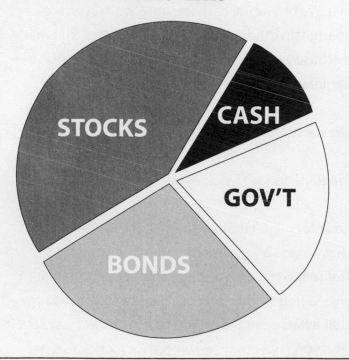

This is a hypothetical illustration to demonstrate the principle of diversification. It is not representative of the past or future results of any specific investment.

And what do we do with that money?

We buy the asset class that now has too small a portion — in this case, the cash portion of our portfolio.

Thus, we sell some stock because we have too much of it. We buy some cash because we don't have enough. In other words, we sell the asset that made the most money and we buy the asset that made the least (or maybe even lost) money.

We sell the winner. We buy the loser.

Want me to say that again?

You're thinking that's crazy. Sell the investment that's made a lot of money? Buy the one that's losing money? Imagine coming home from work and saying to your spouse, "Hey, honey! You know that investment that made us a fortune? I just sold it. And you know that one where we lost our shirts? I bought more!"

At first glance, this doesn't seem to make sense — which explains why so few investors do it. But selling your winners and buying your losers is the smartest action you can take. It's counterintuitive, but it's vital to successful investing.

Remember I promised to tell you how to buy low/sell high? Well, I just did.

Actually, I just told you to sell high/buy low. I reversed the phrase, which is why you stumbled over it. But whether you say buy low/sell high, or sell high/buy low, you get the same results.

You don't want to do it. Yet you wonder why you're not more successful at investing.

I'm simply telling you to buy when prices are low and sell when prices are high. You don't know how to do that because you don't know when the price is high or low. That's because you compare an investment's price to its former price and wonder what its future price will be.

I'm telling you not to do that. Instead, compare an investment not to itself but to the other investments in your portfolio. When you do this, your portfolio will tell you what to do. No predictions are required. Your portfolio will automatically tell you one asset is too high in price *relative to your other investments* (because it constitutes a larger portion of your overall portfolio) and another asset is too low in price relative to your other investments.

It's obvious that you don't want to buy (or own) investments that are too high in price, and you do want to buy investments that are suddenly low in price (and, hence, a bargain).

As a consumer, you know this.

You know the time to buy a big-screen TV is when it's on sale. Would you ever tell your spouse, "Sorry, but we can't buy that television now. It's on sale. We have to wait for the sale to be over, so we can buy it when the price is higher."

You go to the store to buy your favorite ice cream. You see it's on sale. You don't buy the one gallon you intended to buy. You buy four.

Investors refuse to behave as intelligently. They want to buy only investments that have made a lot of money lately. If an investment isn't at an all-time high, they don't want it.

No one wants to buy gold at $200 an ounce. But when it reaches $2,000 an ounce, they load up. Later, when it falls to $1,000 and they've lost 50%, they sell and swear never again will they buy gold.

The truth is simple: If you want to make money from investments, you must sell high/buy low. By *strategically rebalancing* (which is what this concept is called), you will spend your investment career selling assets that are higher in price than others and buying assets that are lower in price.

Sell high/buy low. You now know our secret to successful investing.

The Penalty If You Fail to Buy Low/Sell High

I hope you can see the pitfall of failing to buy low/sell high.

In case you don't, I'll elaborate.

Some investors, seeing that some assets have grown in value while others have fallen (or if their entire portfolio is down, as in 2008, and they see that some have fallen less than others), think the smart action is to sell the loser and buy the winner. They want to get rid of the investment that's doing poorly and buy more of the asset that's doing better.

It's easy to fall into this trap. Media types encourage it by interviewing the fund managers who made a lot of money last year. They don't tell you that past performance does not guarantee future results.

Brokers encourage it too. They love to pitch five-star funds (and they don't tell you the ratings change monthly).

Have you ever seen a broker recommend a one-star fund?

Let's say you start out with a diversified portfolio. You then sell the assets that perform poorly and buy more of the asset that has performed well.

Eventually your portfolio might consist of only one asset.

You need to avoid that situation by selling out of asset classes and market sectors as they climb in value and buying more of asset classes and market sectors as they fall in value. If you don't sell high/buy low, you'll wish you did.

The Right Time to Buy Low/Sell High

You now realize the importance of rebalancing.

But when should you do it? You have two choices: time and percentage. Let's take a look.

Rebalancing by Time

We don't rebalance our clients' portfolios this way, but it's easy, works relatively well, and is better than not rebalancing at all.

Simply rebalance on a calendar basis.

Many people rebalance quarterly. Many employer retirement plans and mutual-fund companies will rebalance your account automatically upon request.

It's simple and painless, but not always as effective as you might like. Often, calendar rebalancing forces you to rebalance for no reason.

If you rebalance quarterly, you'll rebalance on June 30 whether the portfolio needs it or not. And you may often miss opportunities in between, when rebalancing would be beneficial.

For instance, a short-term anomaly might cause an asset class to jump in price momentarily on April 12.

A quick sale of high-priced assets and a purchase of low-cost assets would have locked in your gains. But calendar rebalancing will miss it.

Thus rebalancing by time can cause you to rebalance when you don't need to and miss opportunities that don't coincide with your preset date.

Rebalancing by Percentage

This explains why my firm doesn't rebalance our clients' portfolios according to the calendar. Instead we track each client's individual portfolio.

We begin by providing each client with his or her target asset allocation. For instance, we might designate that a client place 10% of the portfolio into a given asset class. We'll allow the value of that asset class to drift up or down within a certain range — perhaps as high as 12% or as low as 8%. But if the asset's holdings cross either threshold, a rebalance will occur.

Thus we rebalance only and whenever it is needed.

The problem with rebalancing by percentage is that we never know when an asset is about to cross its threshold. We solve that problem by monitoring each client's account every day.

That's cumbersome, which may explain why most consumers don't do it for themselves. It's one reason why consumers choose to hire us. They know rebalancing is important, but it's also a chore. So they happily delegate the task to us.

Normally, a properly designed portfolio should need to be rebalanced only one to four times per year. But in unusually volatile markets, such as those we experienced in 2008, rebalancing a dozen times or more might need to occur.

Rebalancing when needed is designed to help you reduce the fluctuations in value your portfolio experiences, reduce your investment risks, and improve your returns.

So rebalance.

Do it by time or do it by percentage. But do it.

SEVEN

What If You're Already Retired?

If you're already retired, you're shaking your head in dismay.

Sure, I've told you some great things about diversification and long-term investing. But you don't have a long term to invest.

If you are already retired or about to be, your perspective is not the same as people in their twenties, thirties, forties, or fifties.

But what you've read offers lessons for you as well.

Too often people near or in retirement place all their money into bank accounts. As we've seen, they fear risk, need safety, and want income. So they put their money into CDs, bonds, and U.S. Treasuries, and they spend the income those investments generate.

That's a problem. A big problem. But it takes years for people to realize that. Consider the interest rate on a one-year CD. If you invested $100,000 in that CD in 1990, you would have earned $6,800 in interest.[20] But in 2015, you would need more than $12,500 to buy the same goods and services due to 2.5% average annual inflation during that period.[21]

Yet one-year CDs in December 2015 were paying just $270 on $100,000 invested.[22]

That's scary.

This is the challenge you face as a retiree. As a retiree, you need income now. But you also need income in the future. Thus it's not enough for your principal to generate current income. Your principal must also rise so it can generate more income in the future to offset inflation.

Too often retirees emphasize their need for current income without regard for their future needs.

Don't make this mistake.

Don't let your parents make this mistake.

Don't let your grandparents make this mistake.

Don't place your life's savings into low-yielding accounts where the principal balance can't grow. Otherwise, you run the very real risk of running out of money in your elder years.

We deal with this issue every day in my firm because about 40% of our clients are retired. So a substantial portion of our practice is devoted to helping thousands of people deal with the question "How can I live comfortably on my life's savings?"

Our solution for them is called a Systematic Withdrawal Plan (SWP).

This strategy offers our clients the opportunity to generate not only current income but an increased income that keeps pace with inflation and the cost of living.

It's easy: Simply construct a diversified portfolio, and reinvest all interest and dividends.

To compensate for the fact that you've given up the income, you simply arrange to receive a similar monthly amount from your account.

As I explain more fully in my book, *The Truth About Retirement Plans and IRAs*, the SWP has a potential to generate the income you need from your portfolio, with great consistency.

EIGHT

The Most Important Part of the Secret

So the secret is out. Diversification.

You get it. You agree with it. And you already do it.

Or at least you think you do.

People often tell me they are diversified. They brag that they own ten — count 'em, *ten* — mutual funds.

It ain't so much the things we don't know that get us in trouble. It's the things we know that ain't so.

—Artemus Ward

A fellow once showed me his account statements. He was very proud of himself because he had *80* mutual funds. He told me he was "highly diversified." (I wrote about him in *Discover the Wealth Within You*.)

A close look revealed he owned eight money market funds, 23 government bond funds, and 49 U.S. stock funds. But not a single foreign stock fund. No real estate. No natural resources.

Forty-nine stock funds? Every one of them owned shares of Microsoft!

He wasn't diversified.

He was redundant.

Let me show you what diversification really looks like. Look at Figure 8.1.

FIGURE
8.1

Sample Diversified Portfolio

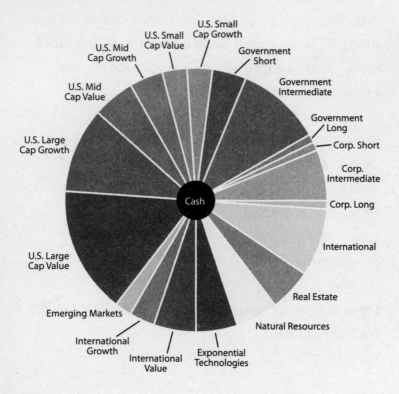

Sources: Morningstar. Past performance does not guarantee future results.

A truly diversified portfolio will own U.S. stocks: large companies, midsize companies, and small companies, broken down by growth and value sectors.

It will own foreign stocks, including emerging markets.

It will own bonds, government and corporate, U.S. and foreign, each sector including short term, intermediate, and long term, and — for the corporate portion — high quality and high yield.

It will own real estate: commercial, residential, retail, industrial, and agricultural, all geographically dispersed.

It will own natural resources, including oil and gas, minerals and precious metals, exponential technologies, and commodities.

A truly diversified portfolio will own it all, all the time!

Anyway, that's how we do it in our firm's practice. Our clients' portfolios typically feature 20 asset classes and market sectors from the global financial marketplace. They typically own upwards of 10,000 stocks from 40 countries.

And they do it by owning just four to 22 funds.

Surprised we don't buy individual stocks and bonds? Too risky for us. Too risky for our clients.

For the five years preceding December 31, 2015, as shown in Figure 8.2, only 49% of all stocks listed on the New York Stock Exchange made money.[23]

During that same period, 99% of mutual funds made money.[24]

And as Figure 8.3 shows, the average return of mutual funds was 9.8% during this period,[25] while the average individual stock *fell* 6.5%.[26]

The reason funds have lower risks and higher returns is simple.

Funds are diversified.

Even the worst of them own dozens of securities, while the best own thousands.

That's why we invest in funds for our clients.

Simple.

Easy.

And you can do it too.

But we don't use retail mutual funds for the Edelman Managed Asset Program®.

Instead, my firm recommends exchange-traded funds and institutional shares for our clients.

It wasn't always this way.

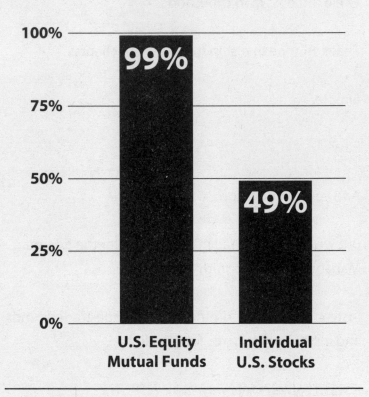

Portion That Were Profitable
2011–2015

| | 99% | 49% |

(U.S. Equity Mutual Funds: 99%; Individual U.S. Stocks: 49%)

Sources: Morningstar. Past performance does not guarantee future results.

FIGURE
8.3

Average Annual Return
2011–2015

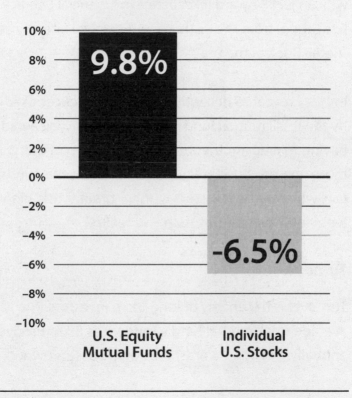

Sources: Morningstar. Past performance does not guarantee future results.

In past decades, we used to recommend traditional retail mutual funds. Why we don't anymore, and how we went about making the conversion, is explained in great detail in my book, *The Lies About Money*, which won the Gold Medal for personal finance in 2008 from the Axiom Business Book Awards. And in 2009, it won an EIFLE Award (Excellence in Financial Literacy Education) from the Institute for Financial Literacy as "Retail Book of the Year."

In *Lies*, I reveal 25 deceptive business practices used by the retail mutual fund industry. To help you avoid having to read another book, here are two of the more onerous business practices retail mutual funds use, which cause investors to incur greater risk, higher fees, and lower returns than you realize.

Turnover

Turnover is the enemy of long-term investors. The average stock mutual fund experiences 80% turnover annually.[27] In other words, 80% of the assets owned by the fund on January 1 are sold during the year and replaced with new assets.

It's ironic. You consider yourself a long-term investor. But if your mutual fund is flipping 80% of your assets annually, your fund has converted you into a short-term trader!

All that trading forces you to pay more taxes. That's because trading triggers short-term capital gains, which you must pay at your maximum tax rate. It will come in the way of IRS Form 1099, which the retail fund company will send you. You'll have to pay as much as 56.7% in federal and state income taxes, even if you reinvest the distributions back into the fund.

Remember how volatile the markets were in 2008? Amid that volatility, many retail mutual funds made distributions equal to 20% or more of their assets. Anyone with $100,000 in such a fund could have incurred $7,000 or more in taxes.

And that's not all.

Fees

All that trading also increases your costs.

After all, someone has to pay the brokerage commissions when your fund buys or sells a security. This is one reason why investors of retail mutual funds pay high fees.

Yet, amazingly, most consumers think they don't pay any fees to own their mutual funds. That's what AARP discovered in 2011 when it surveyed workers around the country. An astonishing 71% said they don't pay any fees to own the mutual funds in their 401(k) and other workplace retirement plans.

Who do they think is paying for the fund company to issue statements and provide toll-free telephone numbers and staff to answer those phone calls? Clearly there are fees involved. It's just that the fees aren't obvious.

They aren't obvious because they aren't on your statement.

If your bank charges you a fee, that fee appears on your statement. When you buy a car, you know how much you're paying. Even your mortgage statement shows you how much of your payment is going toward interest on the loan.

But mutual fund fees don't appear on your statement. The statement shows only the number of shares you own and the share price.

But never the fee.

No wonder so many consumers think they aren't paying anything to own their mutual funds.

Of course there is a fee, called the annual expense ratio. The average for all retail mutual funds is 1.19% per year, according to Morningstar.

But don't look for this information on your statement; it isn't there. You'll have to read the prospectus to find it.

The expense ratio covers the routine costs of fund operations: staff, facilities, marketing, and so on. It does not include the costs of trading. *That* expense is found in another document called the Statement of Additional Information. The average retail mutual fund charges 1.44% annually in trading expenses, according to a 2013 study published in the *Financial Analysts Journal*.[28]

In all, you're paying the average retail mutual fund 2.63% per year. Based on the stock market's average annual return of 9.6% a year,[29] that means you're giving away 27% of your profits on an annual basis.

Imagine giving a waiter a 27% tip.

This might explain why so many members of the Forbes 400 (the wealthiest people in America) are the founders or owners of big mutual-fund companies.

Ned and Abby Johnson, whose family owns Fidelity Investments, are worth $22 billion, according to the 2015 *Forbes* list.

Charlie and Rupert Johnson (no relation to Ned and Abby) are worth $10 billion. They own the Franklin Templeton mutual fund family.

Bill Gross of Janus Funds is worth about $2 billion.

FIGURE
8.4

Name	Is Worth	Largely because of an ownership stake in:
Abigail Johnson	$14.2 billion	Fidelity
Edward Johnson III	$7.8 billion	Fidelity
Charles Johnson	$5.3 billion	Franklin Templeton
Rupert Johnson Jr.	$4.7 billion	Franklin Templeton
Bill Gross	$2.3 billion	PIMCO Funds
Ron Baron	$2.2 billion	Baron Funds
John Calamos	$2 billion	Calamos Funds
Michael Price	$1.7 billion	Mutual Series
Tom Marsico	$1.5 billion	Marsico Funds

The U.S. retail mutual fund industry had nearly $16 trillion in assets at year-end 2014 (the latest data available), according to the Investment Company Institute. U.S. stock and bond mutual funds charge $420.8 billion in fees each year. No wonder these guys are among the wealthiest people in America.

Turnover and fees are just two of the 25 deceptive business practices used by the retail mutual fund industry. That's why we say no to them.

Instead we use institutional mutual funds and exchange-traded funds. Most folks are unaware of these investments, yet they represent the solution to the deceptive and manipulative business practices of the retail mutual fund world.

Now, you might be a little confused. I just told you to say no to retail mutual funds, and now I'm recommending institutional mutual funds. Let me explain the difference.

An institutional fund is typically marketed to institutions and often requires you to invest millions of dollars. That's why you've never heard of them. As a retail investor working with a retail advisor at a retail brokerage firm, you don't have access to them.

You see, others with billions of dollars to invest approach the investment decision differently from those of us who have, say, smaller amounts of money.

Here's what I mean. Imagine I give $1,000 to you and another $1,000 to your friend. I send you both to Walmart with only one instruction: You must both spend all the money. Will you and your friend emerge with the same merchandise?

With more than 117,000 products in the store and a million items for sale online,[30] probably not.

So let's change the rules. I send you both back to Walmart. But this time you each get $1 billion. Now will you both emerge with the same merchandise?

You certainly will.

After all, with $1 billion at your disposal, it's no longer a question of what to buy. You have no choice but to buy everything.

This is the dilemma faced by David Swensen. He's the manager of the Yale Endowment Fund, a $22 billion portfolio.[31]

He doesn't have the luxury of deciding whether to buy Coca-Cola or Pepsi. With $22 billion to spend, he must buy both.

Thus for the David Swensens of the financial world, the decision is not which stock to buy but how much money to put into stocks in the first place — as opposed to bonds, real estate, gold, or oil and gas.

For David Swensen, what matters is the question of asset allocation.

As a result, institutional funds are very consistent in their holdings.

They engage in little turnover because there's nothing left to buy. Thus, expenses are lower, and so is your annual tax liability.

There are other cost savings too. If you're going to buy everything, you don't need a high-priced portfolio manager backed by a team of security analysts. All you need is a clerk to handle the transactions.

Although many institutional funds are not available to retail investors like you, some are. And there's another type of investment that also lets you enjoy a market-based (rather than manager-based) investment approach. They're called exchange-traded funds, and my firm provides these to our clients in addition to institutional funds.

ETFs have been around since 1993. Like institutional funds, they're up to 90% cheaper than the average retail mutual fund. ETFs trade on the New York Stock Exchange, meaning you buy them from a brokerage firm.

Because ETFs trade via brokerage accounts, they cost much less to operate. They pass the savings to you.

Conclusion

So now you know our secret to successful investing. Build a highly diversified portfolio consisting of low-cost institutional shares and exchange-traded funds. Buy low/sell high through strategic rebalancing, and maintain a long-term investment horizon.

That's all there is to it.

If you prefer, you can do this yourself, or you can retain a financial advisor to handle it for you.

If you know how to construct a portfolio and research the investments for it, you might consider doing it yourself. You'll need to monitor the portfolio to execute rebalances as needed, and you'll have to handle your own paperwork and record-keeping for tax purposes. You'll also need to wrap this entire effort into the financial planning process, taking into consideration college, retirement, and estate planning; home ownership and mortgages; credit and debt; employee benefits; Social Security; insurance; taxes; and more. Note that we didn't cover any of these topics in this book; you'll need to read my others for that information.

If you prefer not to spend your time on all that, you'll want to delegate these chores to an advisor. That pretty much describes the kind of people who hire financial planning and investment management firms like ours. Our clients know they need a proper investment strategy, but they don't want to do it themselves. If you turn to a firm like ours, we handle everything for you. Other firms provide similar services. So the choice is yours.

So do it yourself or hire someone to do it for you.

But do it.

And remember back in Chapter 1 when I told you about the one major investment goal you should have?

That goal, as you recall, is financial security, and following the advice provided in this book can help you achieve the financial security you want for yourself and your family.

Ric's Recipe

Prep time: the long term (at least 5 years)

Serves: your entire family with heaping portions of financial security

What You'll Need:

1 Cup of Media Advice

1 Pinch of Investment Fads

1 Cup of High-Cost Mutual Funds

1 Dash of Blue-Chip Stocks

2 Teaspoons of ETFs

1 Tablespoon of Institutional Shares

Take a knife to your high-cost retail mutual funds and chop them into little pieces. Repeat with the media advice, investment fads, and blue-chip stocks. Combine with the chopped funds and discard.

In a clean pan, combine ETFs with institutional shares. Cover and let simmer for a long time. Rebalance periodically. At retirement, enjoy!

Illustration by Wendy Sefcik

Notes

1. Standard & Poor's.

2. Consumer Price Index for All Urban Consumers: All Items Year-over-Year Change — Data Series Monthly January 1926–December 2015. Source: Bureau of Labor Statistics.

3. TrimTabs Investment Research.

4. Charles Mackay, *Extraordinary Popular Delusions and the Madness of Crowds*. Published in 1852.

5. Investopedia.

6. Dow Jones & Company.

7. Bloomberg.

8. NASDAQ (National Association of Securities Dealers Automated Quotations).

9. NASDAQ; Ibbotson Associates.

10. S&P/Case-Shiller Composite Home Index and National Association of Realtors.

11. Congressional Budget Office: Estimated Impact of Automatic Budget Enforcement Procedures Specified in the Budget Control Act.

12. *MarketWatch*.

13. Dow Jones & Company.

14. Bing Liang, "Price Pressure: Evidence from the 'Dartboard' Column." *The Journal of Business* 72, no. 1 (January 1999): 119–134.

15. Michaela Pagel, "Overwhelmed with Your Retirement Portfolio? Paying Less Attention Now May Pay Off in Larger Returns in the Future." Columbia Business School via PRNewswire, January 7, 2015. http://www.prnewswire.com/news-releases/overwhelmed-with-your-retirement-portfolio-paying-less-attention-now-may-pay-off-in-larger-returns-in-the-future-300017294.html

16. Ibbotson Associates.

17. Morningstar Direct.

18. Ibbotson Associates.

19. National Bureau of Economic Research.

20. Ibbotson Associates.

21. Ibbotson Associates.

22. The average one-year CD rate according to Bankrate.com as of January 1, 2016.

23. Morningstar.

24. Morningstar.

25. Morningstar.

26. Morningstar.

27. Morningstar.

28. Roger Edelen, Richard Evans, and Gregory Kadlec, "Shedding Light on 'Invisible' Costs: Trading Costs and Mutual Fund Performance." *Financial Analysts Journal* 69, no. 1 (January/February 2013): 33–44.

29. Performance of the S&P 500, 1926–2015, according to Ibbotson Associates.

30. Hayley Peterson, "Walmart Is Making 2 Major Changes to Its Stores." October 26, 2015.

31. Yale University.

Index

Page numbers in **bold** refer to figures.

The Other Side of Money
By Jean Edelman

**Living a More Balanced Life
Through 52 Weekly Inspirations**

The Personal Side of Personal Finance
So much of our lives is focused on, or affected by, dollars. But too much attention to money can actually interfere with our wish to live a happy, fulfilling life. That's why personal finance is more personal than finance.

The Other Side of Money helps us reflect on how we are living our lives and suggests how we can see people and the world around us in a positive, loving way. From life's simple issues to our bigger questions, *The Other Side of Money* helps us find quiet and balance by turning inward so we can be in the moment. By looking at how we live our lives, we discover the lessons that let us become better people.

Ready to get started?
We're ready to help you.

We know how hard it can be to find the right personal financial advisor. Decades ago, Ric and Jean Edelman sought financial advice, but what they got was very disappointing. So they decided to teach themselves about personal finance, and then they created an advisory firm so they could share what they learned with others.

Today, Edelman Financial Services is one of the largest independent financial planning and investment management firms in America[1], serving more than 30,000 individuals and families, with nearly $16 billion in assets under management.[2] We are ready to help you too, both online and via 40+ offices across the country. Come learn what so many others have discovered, and see how we can help you achieve all your financial goals.

EDELMAN
FINANCIAL SERVICES

About the Author

Acclaimed Financial Advisor

Ric is one of the nation's most recognized financial advisors. He was named one of the "10 most influential figures" in the investment advisory field[1] and among the "15 most transformative people in the industry" by InvestmentNews,[2] and voted by readers of *Wealth Management* as one of the "four most influential people in the financial services field."[3] He was three times named the #1 Independent Financial Advisor by *Barron's*.[4]

Bestselling Author, Radio and TV Host, and Educator

Ric is a #1 *New York Times* bestselling author. With more than 1 million copies collectively in print, his eight books on personal finance have been translated into several languages and educated countless people worldwide. Ric's radio show has been on the air for more than 25 years and is heard throughout the country. For three years in a row, Ric has been named one of the 100 top radio talk show hosts by *Talkers* magazine[5] and in 2012 was named the #2 most important weekend-only talk show host in the nation.

Ric also publishes an award-winning 16-page monthly newsletter, offers personal finance education at RicEdelman.com, and speaks frequently at industry conferences.

Philanthropic Activities

Ric and Jean Edelman are major supporters of the Edelman Planetarium at Rowan University and the Edelman Nursing Career Development Center at the Inova Health System.

Through donations and service as board members and volunteers, they support many other charities and nonprofit organizations, including the Boys & Girls Clubs of America, American Savings Education Council, and the Jump$tart Coalition for Personal Financial Literacy.

[1] The RIABiz listing of the 10 most influential figures in the Registered Investment Advisor industry is in recognition of notable, driven and influential executives who are advancing their firms and are considered to be influential in the RIA business. Investor experience/returns were not considered as part of this ranking.

[2] InvestmentNews 15th Anniversary Issue. June 23, 2013

[3] WealthManagement.com/WealthManagement Madness, March 2014.

[4] According to *Barron's*, "The formula [used] to rank advisors has three major components: assets managed, revenue produced and quality of the advisor's practice. Investment returns are not a component of the rankings because an advisor's returns are dictated largely by each client's risk tolerance. The quality-of-practice component includes an evaluation of each advisor's regulatory record." The rankings are based on the universe of applications submitted to *Barron's*. The selection process begins with a nomination and application provided to *Barron's*. Principals of Edelman Financial Services, LLC self-nominated the firm and submitted quantitative and qualitative information to *Barron's* as requested. *Barron's* reviewed and considered this information which resulted in the rankings on Aug. 27, 2012/Aug. 28, 2010/Aug. 31, 2009.

[5] *Talkers* Magazine "Heavy Hundred" ranking is based on a number of both quantitative and qualitative criteria and is determined by collective analysis of the *Talkers* editorial board with input from a wide variety of industry leaders. Investor experience/returns were not considered as part of this ranking.

Ric Edelman, Founder and Executive Chairman of Edelman Financial Services, LLC, a Registered Investment Advisor, is an Investment Advisor Representative who offers advisory services through EFS and is a Registered Representative and Registered Principal of, and offers securities through, EF Legacy Securities, LLC, an affiliated broker/dealer, member FINRA/SIPC.